CONTENTS

INTRODUCTION

"Toxic Love: A Guide to Recognizing and Healing from Unhealthy Relationships" is a comprehensive book that aims to help readers identify and navigate toxic relationships. With a focus on understanding the signs and behaviors of toxic relationships, this book provides valuable insights into the impact of such relationships on mental health and self-esteem. It also offers practical guidance on setting boundaries, ending toxic relationships, and healing from the aftermath. Whether you are currently in a toxic relationship or have recently ended one, this book will empower you to recognize the red flags, prioritize your well-being, and build healthier relationships in the future.

In the first section of the book, "Understanding Toxic Relationships," readers will gain a clear understanding of what constitutes a toxic relationship and the common signs to look out for. The chapter delves into different types of toxic relationships and explores the detrimental effects they can have on mental health. By providing a solid foundation of knowledge, readers will be equipped to recognize and acknowledge the toxic dynamics in their own relationships.

The subsequent chapters focus on specific aspects of toxic relationships, such as recognizing toxic behaviors, understanding codependency, exploring unhealthy relationship patterns, and the impact of toxic relationships on self-esteem. The book also offers practical advice on healing from a toxic relationship, setting boundaries, ending the relationship, and navigating co-parenting in a toxic environment. Additionally, readers will find guidance on building healthy relationships, practicing self-love and self-care, and moving forward to create a fulfilling and thriving life. With its comprehensive approach and practical strategies, "Toxic Love" is an essential guide for anyone seeking to break free from the cycle of unhealthy relationships and find healing and happiness.

CHAPTER 1: UNDERSTANDING TOXIC RELATIONSHIPS

Defining Toxic Relationships

Toxic relationships are characterized by unhealthy and harmful dynamics that can have a detrimental impact on our well-being. These relationships are often characterized by a lack of respect, trust, and support, and can leave individuals feeling drained, unhappy, and emotionally depleted. It is important to understand and define toxic relationships in order to recognize and address them effectively.

A toxic relationship can be defined as a relationship that consistently brings more harm than good to one or both individuals involved. It is a relationship that is marked by negativity, manipulation, control, and a lack of healthy communication and boundaries. Toxic relationships can occur in various contexts, including romantic partnerships, friendships, family relationships, and even professional relationships.

In a toxic relationship, there is often a power imbalance, with one person exerting control and dominance over the other. This can manifest in different ways, such as through emotional manipulation, verbal abuse, physical or sexual violence, or constant criticism and belittlement. The toxic person may use tactics such as gaslighting, where they manipulate the other person's perception of reality, making them doubt their own thoughts, feelings, and experiences.

It is important to note that toxic relationships are not always easy to identify, especially in the early stages. In fact, toxic behaviors may be disguised as love, concern, or protection, making it difficult for the person experiencing them to recognize the toxicity. However, there are common signs and patterns that can help individuals identify whether they are in a toxic relationship.

Recognizing the signs of a toxic relationship is crucial for understanding and addressing the issue. Here are some common signs that may indicate a toxic relationship:

1. Lack of respect and support: In a toxic relationship, there is often a lack of respect for each other's boundaries, opinions, and feelings. One person may consistently dismiss or invalidate the other's thoughts and emotions, leaving them feeling unheard and unvalued.
2. Constant criticism and belittlement: Toxic relationships are often characterized by a pattern of constant criticism, belittlement, and humiliation. The toxic person may use derogatory language, insults, or sarcasm to undermine the other person's self-esteem and confidence.
3. Manipulation and control: Toxic relationships thrive on manipulation and control. The toxic person

may use tactics such as guilt-tripping, emotional blackmail, or threats to manipulate the other person's behavior and choices. They may also try to isolate the individual from their support system, making them dependent on the toxic person for validation and approval.

4. Lack of trust and honesty: Trust is a fundamental aspect of any healthy relationship. In a toxic relationship, there is often a lack of trust and honesty. The toxic person may lie, deceive, or betray the other person's trust, leading to feelings of insecurity and doubt.

5. Emotional and physical abuse: Toxic relationships can involve various forms of abuse, including emotional, verbal, physical, and sexual abuse. Emotional abuse can manifest as constant criticism, humiliation, and manipulation, while physical abuse involves acts of violence or aggression. Sexual abuse refers to any non-consensual sexual activity or coercion.

6. Constant drama and conflict: Toxic relationships are often characterized by a cycle of constant drama and conflict. Arguments and disagreements may escalate quickly and become emotionally or physically abusive. The toxic person may thrive on creating chaos and thrive on the power dynamics that come with it.

7. Feeling drained and unhappy: One of the most telling signs of a toxic relationship is the consistent feeling of being drained, unhappy, and emotionally depleted. Toxic relationships can take a toll on one's mental and emotional well-being, leaving them feeling exhausted, anxious, and depressed.

It is important to remember that not all relationships are perfect, and occasional disagreements or conflicts are normal. However, if these signs are consistently present in your relationship and are causing you distress, it may be an indication of a toxic relationship. Recognizing and acknowledging the toxicity is the first step towards healing and creating healthier relationships in the future.

———

Common Signs of a Toxic Relationship

Recognizing a toxic relationship can be challenging, especially when you are emotionally invested in the person or situation. However, it is crucial to be aware of the signs that indicate a relationship may be toxic. By understanding these signs, you can take steps to protect yourself and make informed decisions about your well-being. Here are some common signs of a toxic relationship:

In a healthy relationship, trust and respect are the foundation. However, in a toxic relationship, these qualities may be absent or severely compromised. You may find that your partner consistently breaks promises, lies, or engages in secretive behavior. They may also disrespect your boundaries, dismiss your feelings, or belittle your achievements. If you feel constantly on edge or disrespected in your relationship, it may be a sign of toxicity.

Toxic relationships often involve a pattern of constant criticism and negativity. Your partner may frequently put you down, make hurtful comments, or undermine your self-esteem. They may focus on your flaws and shortcomings, rather than supporting and uplifting you. This constant negativity can erode your self-confidence and leave you feeling emotionally drained.

One of the most significant signs of a toxic relationship is control and manipulation. Your partner may try to control your every move, dictate who you can spend time with, or isolate you from friends and family.

They may use manipulation tactics such as guilt-tripping, gaslighting, or emotional blackmail to maintain power and control over you. If you feel like you are constantly walking on eggshells or have lost your sense of autonomy, it may be a sign of a toxic relationship.

Healthy relationships thrive on open and honest communication, as well as emotional intimacy. In a toxic relationship, communication may be lacking or filled with conflict. Your partner may avoid discussing important issues, dismiss your concerns, or refuse to take responsibility for their actions. Emotional intimacy may also be absent, leaving you feeling disconnected and unfulfilled in the relationship.

Toxic relationships often involve imbalanced power dynamics, where one partner holds more power and control over the other. This power imbalance can manifest in various ways, such as financial control, decision-making dominance, or physical and emotional abuse. If you feel like you have little say in the relationship or are constantly being overpowered, it may be a sign of a toxic dynamic.

Toxic relationships are often characterized by a constant cycle of drama and volatility. Arguments may escalate quickly, and conflicts may become explosive and unpredictable. Your partner may thrive on creating chaos or thrive on the emotional rollercoaster. This constant state of turmoil can be emotionally exhausting and detrimental to your well-being.

In a healthy relationship, both partners support and empathize with each other's needs and emotions. However, in a toxic relationship, your partner may lack empathy and fail to provide the support you need. They may dismiss your feelings, minimize your experiences, or invalidate your emotions. This lack of support can leave you feeling isolated and emotionally neglected.

One of the most alarming signs of a toxic relationship is the presence of fear and intimidation. Your partner may use threats, physical violence, or coercive tactics to control and intimidate you. Feeling afraid or unsafe in your relationship is a clear indication of toxicity, and it is essential to seek help and support to ensure your safety.

Recognizing these signs is the first step towards acknowledging that you are in a toxic relationship. It is important to remember that no one deserves to be in a toxic relationship, and you have the right to prioritize your well-being. If you identify with any of these signs, it may be time to seek support and consider taking steps towards healing and finding a healthier relationship.

———

Types of Toxic Relationships

Toxic relationships come in various forms and can manifest in different ways. It is important to understand the different types of toxic relationships in order to recognize and address them effectively. Here are some common types of toxic relationships:

Controlling and manipulative relationships are characterized by one partner exerting power and control over the other. The controlling partner may use tactics such as manipulation, coercion, and intimidation to maintain dominance and influence the thoughts, feelings, and actions of their partner. They may isolate their partner from friends and family, monitor their activities, and make all the decisions in the relationship. This type of toxic relationship can be emotionally and psychologically damaging, leaving the victim feeling trapped and powerless.

Emotionally abusive relationships involve a pattern of behavior where one partner consistently belittles, humiliates, and undermines the other's self-worth and emotional well-being. Emotional abuse can take many forms, including constant criticism, insults, gaslighting, and withholding affection or support. The abuser may manipulate their partner's emotions, making them feel guilty, ashamed, or responsible for the abuse. Over time, the victim may lose their sense of self and become dependent on the abuser for validation and approval.

Physically and sexually abusive relationships involve the use of physical force or coercion to control and dominate the partner. Physical abuse can include hitting, punching, kicking, or any form of physical harm. Sexual abuse involves any non-consensual sexual activity or manipulation. These types of toxic relationships are extremely dangerous and can have severe physical and psychological consequences for the victim. It is important to seek immediate help and support if you are in a physically or sexually abusive relationship.

Narcissistic relationships are characterized by one partner who has an excessive sense of self-importance and a constant need for admiration and attention. They often lack empathy and have a sense of entitlement, using others for their own gain. In a narcissistic relationship, the narcissistic partner may manipulate, exploit, and devalue their partner to maintain their own inflated sense of self-worth. They may engage in gaslighting, where they distort the truth and make their partner doubt their own reality. Being in a relationship with a narcissist can be emotionally draining and damaging to one's self-esteem.

Codependent relationships are characterized by an unhealthy reliance on each other for emotional support and validation. In a codependent relationship, one partner may have low self-esteem and seek validation and approval from the other. The other partner may have a need to feel needed and may enable the codepend behavior. This dynamic can be toxic as it perpetuates unhealthy patterns of dependency and can lead to a lack of personal boundaries and individual growth.

Addictive relationships involve one or both partners being addicted to substances or behaviors that negatively impact the relationship. This can include addictions to drugs, alcohol, gambling, or even work. In addictive relationships, the addiction takes precedence over the well-being of the individuals and the relationship itself. The addictive behavior can lead to neglect, abuse, and a breakdown of trust and communication.

Recognizing the type of toxic relationship you are in is the first step towards healing and breaking free from its harmful effects. It is important to remember that no one deserves to be in a toxic relationship, and seeking support from friends, family, or professionals can help you navigate the process of healing and moving towards healthier relationships.

———

The Impact of Toxic Relationships on Mental Health

Toxic relationships can have a profound impact on our mental health. When we are involved in a toxic relationship, it can slowly erode our sense of self-worth, happiness, and overall well-being. The negative effects of toxic relationships can manifest in various ways, affecting our emotional, psychological, and even physical health.

One of the most significant impacts of toxic relationships on mental health is the emotional distress they cause. Toxic relationships are often characterized by constant criticism, belittling, and emotional manipulation. This can lead to feelings of anxiety, depression, and low self-esteem. The constant negativity and emotional abuse can wear down our mental resilience, leaving us feeling emotionally drained and overwhelmed.

Being in a toxic relationship can significantly increase our stress levels. Toxic partners often create an environment of constant tension and conflict. They may engage in controlling behaviors, create unrealistic expectations, or constantly criticize and demean us. This chronic stress can lead to physical symptoms such as headaches, digestive issues, and sleep disturbances. It can also contribute to the development of mental health disorders such as anxiety and depression.

Toxic relationships often involve isolating behaviors from the toxic partner. They may discourage or prevent us from spending time with friends and family, or they may actively try to turn those close to us against us. This isolation can lead to feelings of loneliness and a lack of support. Without a strong support system, it becomes even more challenging to cope with the negative effects of the toxic relationship, further impacting our mental health.

Toxic partners often engage in gaslighting and manipulation, making us doubt our own perceptions and experiences. They may twist the truth, deny their harmful behaviors, or blame us for their actions. Over time, this can lead to a loss of trust in ourselves and our ability to make sound judgments. We may start to question our own sanity and constantly second-guess our thoughts and feelings. This self-doubt and self-blame can have a significant impact on our mental well-being, leading to feelings of confusion, guilt, and shame.

Being in a toxic relationship can distort our self-image and self-worth. Toxic partners often engage in constant criticism and put-downs, making us believe that we are unworthy or unlovable. This negative messaging can seep into our subconscious, leading to a distorted perception of ourselves. We may start to believe that we deserve the mistreatment or that we are incapable of finding a healthy and loving relationship. This negative self-image can have long-lasting effects on our mental health, contributing to feelings of worthlessness and self-destructive behaviors.

The cumulative effects of toxic relationships can contribute to the development or exacerbation of anxiety and depression. The constant stress, emotional abuse, and feelings of isolation can take a toll on our mental well-being. We may experience persistent feelings of sadness, hopelessness, and a general lack of interest in activities we once enjoyed. Anxiety may manifest as excessive worry, restlessness, and a constant sense of unease. It is essential to recognize the connection between toxic relationships and mental health disorders and seek appropriate support and treatment.

In some cases, the impact of a toxic relationship can be so severe that it leads to the development of post-traumatic stress disorder (PTSD). PTSD can occur when we have experienced or witnessed a traumatic event, such as ongoing emotional or physical abuse. Symptoms of PTSD may include intrusive thoughts, flashbacks, nightmares, hypervigilance, and avoidance of triggers associated with the traumatic experience. It is crucial to seek professional help if you suspect you may be experiencing symptoms of PTSD as a result of a toxic relationship.

In conclusion, toxic relationships can have a devastating impact on our mental health. The emotional distress, increased stress levels, isolation, self-doubt, negative self-image, and the development of anxiety, depression, and even PTSD are all potential consequences of being in a toxic relationship. Recognizing the impact of toxic relationships on our mental health is the first step towards healing and breaking free from these harmful dynamics. Seeking support from trusted friends, family, or mental health professionals can provide the necessary guidance and resources to navigate the healing process. Remember, you deserve to be in a healthy and loving relationship that nurtures your mental well-being.

CHAPTER 2: RECOGNIZING TOXIC BEHAVIORS

Manipulation and Control

Manipulation and control are two key behaviors that are often present in toxic relationships. These behaviors can be subtle and insidious, making it difficult for the victim to recognize them. In this section, we will explore the signs of manipulation and control in a relationship and provide guidance on how to recognize these toxic behaviors.

Manipulation is a tactic used by one person to control and influence another person's thoughts, feelings, and actions. It is a form of emotional abuse that can be damaging to the victim's self-esteem and overall well-being. Here are some common signs of manipulation in a relationship:

1. Gaslighting: Gaslighting is a manipulative technique where the abuser makes the victim doubt their own reality. They may deny or distort events, manipulate facts, or make the victim question their memory or sanity. Gaslighting can leave the victim feeling

confused, insecure, and powerless.

2. Guilt-tripping: Manipulators often use guilt as a way to control their partner. They may make the victim feel responsible for their unhappiness or use emotional blackmail to get what they want. This can lead to the victim feeling constantly guilty and obligated to meet the manipulator's demands.

3. Isolation: Manipulators may isolate their partner from friends, family, and support networks. They may discourage or prevent the victim from spending time with loved ones, making them dependent on the manipulator for social interaction and support. This isolation can make it harder for the victim to recognize the toxic nature of the relationship.

4. Emotional blackmail: Manipulators may use emotional blackmail to manipulate their partner's behavior. They may threaten to harm themselves, end the relationship, or withhold love and affection unless their demands are met. This can create a constant state of fear and anxiety for the victim, making it difficult for them to assert their own needs and boundaries.

5. Control over finances: Manipulators may exert control over their partner's finances as a way to maintain power and control. They may restrict access to money, monitor spending, or make all financial decisions without input from the victim. This can leave the victim feeling trapped and financially dependent on the manipulator.

Control is another toxic behavior that can be present in a relationship. It involves one person exerting power and dominance over the other, often through intimidation, coercion, or physical force. Here are some signs of control in a relationship:

1. Jealousy and possessiveness: A controlling partner may exhibit extreme jealousy and possessiveness. They may constantly accuse their partner of infidelity, monitor their activities, or isolate them from friends and family. This behavior is an attempt to control the partner's actions and limit their independence.

2. Monitoring and surveillance: A controlling partner may invade their partner's privacy by constantly checking their phone, emails, or social media accounts. They may also track their partner's whereabouts or demand constant updates on their activities. This invasion of privacy is a way to maintain control and prevent the partner from having any autonomy.

3. Physical and sexual abuse: Control can escalate to physical and sexual abuse in a toxic relationship. The abuser may use physical force, threats, or coercion to exert control over their partner. This behavior is not only physically harmful but also emotionally damaging, leaving the victim feeling trapped and powerless.

4. Micromanaging: A controlling partner may micromanage every aspect of their partner's life, from their appearance to their daily routines. They may dictate what the partner can wear, who they can talk to, or how they should behave. This level of control can be suffocating and leave the victim feeling like they have no autonomy or agency.

5. Manipulation of information: A controlling partner may manipulate information to control the narrative and maintain power. They may distort facts, lie, or withhold information to manipulate their partner's perception of reality. This manipulation of information can make it difficult for the victim to

trust their own judgment and make independent decisions.

Recognizing manipulation and control in a relationship is the first step towards breaking free from a toxic dynamic. It is important to trust your instincts and listen to your feelings. If you suspect that you are in a toxic relationship, reach out to a trusted friend, family member, or professional for support and guidance. Remember, you deserve to be in a healthy and loving relationship.

———

Verbal and Emotional Abuse

Verbal and emotional abuse are two common forms of toxic behavior that can occur within a relationship. While they may not leave visible scars like physical abuse, the impact of these types of abuse can be just as damaging, if not more so. In this section, we will explore what verbal and emotional abuse look like, how they can manifest in a relationship, and the long-term effects they can have on a person's mental and emotional well-being.

Verbal abuse involves the use of words, tone, or language to belittle, demean, or control another person. It can take many forms, including insults, name-calling, yelling, screaming, mocking, or using derogatory language. Verbal abuse can be overt or subtle, but its purpose is always to undermine the victim's self-esteem and sense of self-worth.

Recognizing verbal abuse can be challenging, as it often occurs behind closed doors and may not leave physical evidence. However, there are some common signs that can help you identify if you are experiencing verbal abuse in your relationship:

1. Constant criticism: Your partner consistently

criticizes your appearance, intelligence, abilities, or decisions, making you feel inadequate or worthless.

2. Humiliation and embarrassment: Your partner publicly humiliates or embarrasses you, either in front of others or privately, to exert control and power over you.

3. Blaming and shaming: Your partner blames you for their own mistakes or shortcomings, making you feel responsible for their behavior or emotions.

4. Threats and intimidation: Your partner uses threats, intimidation, or coercion to manipulate and control you, making you fear the consequences of not complying with their demands.

5. Gaslighting: Your partner denies or distorts your reality, making you question your own perceptions, memories, and sanity.

Verbal abuse can have severe and long-lasting effects on a person's mental and emotional well-being. Some of the common effects include:

1. Low self-esteem: Constant criticism and belittlement can erode your self-confidence and self-worth, leading to feelings of inadequacy and self-doubt.

2. Anxiety and depression: Verbal abuse can contribute to the development of anxiety and depression, as the constant negativity and emotional manipulation take a toll on your mental health.

3. Isolation: Verbal abuse often goes hand in hand with isolation, as the abuser may try to control who you interact with and limit your support system.

4. Post-traumatic stress disorder (PTSD): In severe cases, ongoing verbal abuse can lead to symptoms of PTSD, such as flashbacks, nightmares, and hypervigilance.

5. Physical health issues: The chronic stress and emotional turmoil caused by verbal abuse can

manifest in physical symptoms, such as headaches, digestive problems, and weakened immune system.

Emotional abuse is another form of toxic behavior that can be equally damaging to a person's well-being. It involves the manipulation and control of a person's emotions, often through tactics such as manipulation, gaslighting, and invalidation.

Recognizing emotional abuse can be challenging, as it often occurs gradually and subtly. However, there are some common signs that can help you identify if you are experiencing emotional abuse in your relationship:

1. Manipulation and control: Your partner uses manipulation tactics, such as guilt-tripping, emotional blackmail, or withholding affection, to control your thoughts, feelings, and actions.
2. Gaslighting: Your partner denies or distorts your reality, making you question your own perceptions, memories, and sanity.
3. Invalidation: Your partner dismisses or undermines your feelings, experiences, and opinions, making you doubt your own emotions and judgment.
4. Isolation: Your partner isolates you from friends, family, and support networks, making you dependent on them for emotional validation and support.
5. Emotional withholding: Your partner withholds affection, attention, or emotional support as a means of punishment or control.

Emotional abuse can have profound and long-lasting effects on a person's mental and emotional well-being. Some of the common effects include:

1. Low self-esteem: Emotional abuse erodes your self-confidence and self-worth, making you doubt your abilities, decisions, and value as a person.

2. Anxiety and depression: The constant emotional manipulation and invalidation can contribute to the development of anxiety and depression.
3. Difficulty trusting others: Emotional abuse can make it challenging to trust others, as you may fear being hurt or manipulated again.
4. Emotional dysregulation: Emotional abuse can disrupt your ability to regulate your emotions, leading to mood swings, anger, or emotional numbness.
5. Self-blame and guilt: Emotional abuse often leaves victims feeling responsible for the abuser's behavior, leading to self-blame and guilt.

Recognizing and acknowledging verbal and emotional abuse is the first step towards healing and breaking free from a toxic relationship. It is essential to remember that no one deserves to be treated with disrespect or cruelty. Seeking support from trusted friends, family, or professionals can provide the guidance and validation needed to navigate the healing process.

———

Physical and Sexual Abuse

Physical and sexual abuse are two of the most severe forms of toxic behavior that can occur within a relationship. These forms of abuse can have devastating effects on the victim's physical and emotional well-being. It is crucial to recognize the signs of physical and sexual abuse in order to protect yourself or someone you care about from further harm.

Physical abuse involves the use of physical force or violence to cause harm or injury to another person. It can manifest in various ways, including hitting, punching, kicking, slapping, choking, or using weapons. Recognizing physical abuse can be challenging, as it often occurs behind closed doors and the victim may try to hide the evidence or make excuses for their injuries. However, there are some common signs that may indicate the presence of physical abuse:

1. Unexplained injuries: Bruises, cuts, burns, or broken bones that cannot be explained or are inconsistent with the explanations given by the person experiencing them.
2. Frequent visits to the emergency room: If someone you know frequently seeks medical attention for injuries, it may be a sign of physical abuse.
3. Wearing concealing clothing: The person may consistently wear long sleeves or clothing that covers their body, even in warm weather, to hide bruises or other signs of physical abuse.
4. Fearful behavior: The person may exhibit signs of fear or anxiety around their partner, flinching at sudden movements or becoming tense when their partner is present.
5. Isolation: The person may become increasingly isolated from friends and family, as the abuser may try to control their access to support systems.

If you suspect that someone you know is experiencing physical abuse, it is important to approach the situation with sensitivity and empathy. Encourage them to seek help and offer your support. Remember, it is not your responsibility to fix the situation, but you can provide a listening ear and help them access resources such as domestic violence hotlines or local support organizations.

Sexual abuse involves any unwanted sexual activity or behavior imposed on an individual without their consent. It can occur within a relationship, and it is important to understand that consent is an ongoing process that can be withdrawn at any time. Recognizing sexual abuse can be challenging, as it often involves manipulation, coercion, or threats from the abuser.

Here are some signs that may indicate the presence of sexual abuse:

1. Non-consensual sexual acts: If someone is engaging in sexual activities without the explicit consent of their partner, it is a clear sign of sexual abuse.
2. Forced or coerced sexual acts: The person may feel pressured or forced into engaging in sexual activities that they are uncomfortable with or do not want to participate in.
3. Emotional and psychological manipulation: The abuser may use emotional manipulation or threats to coerce the person into engaging in sexual activities against their will.
4. Fear or anxiety around sexual encounters: The person may exhibit signs of fear, anxiety, or distress when it comes to sexual encounters with their partner.
5. Physical signs of abuse: In some cases, sexual abuse may result in physical injuries or trauma, such as bruising, bleeding, or pain in the genital area.

If you suspect that someone you know is experiencing sexual abuse, it is crucial to approach the situation with sensitivity and respect. Encourage them to seek professional help from organizations specializing in sexual assault or domestic violence. It is important to remember that the survivor should never be blamed or questioned about their experience. Offer your support and let them know that they are not alone.

If you are experiencing physical or sexual abuse, it is essential to reach out for help and support. Remember, you are not alone, and there are resources available to assist you in escaping the abusive relationship and beginning the healing process. Here are some steps you can take:

1. Reach out to a trusted friend or family member: Share

your experience with someone you trust and ask for their support. They can provide emotional support and help you access resources.

2. Contact a helpline or support organization: There are numerous helplines and support organizations available that specialize in assisting individuals who have experienced physical or sexual abuse. They can provide guidance, resources, and a safe space to talk about your experiences.

3. Seek professional help: Consider reaching out to a therapist or counselor who specializes in trauma and abuse. They can provide you with the necessary tools and support to heal from the trauma and rebuild your life.

4. Develop a safety plan: If you are planning to leave the abusive relationship, it is important to create a safety plan to ensure your well-being. This may involve finding a safe place to stay, gathering important documents, and informing trusted individuals about your situation.

5. Report the abuse: If you feel safe and comfortable doing so, consider reporting the abuse to the appropriate authorities. They can help ensure your safety and hold the abuser accountable for their actions.

Remember, healing from physical and sexual abuse takes time, and everyone's journey is unique. Be patient with yourself and seek the support you need to begin the healing process. You deserve to live a life free from abuse and to rebuild a future filled with love, respect, and happiness.

———

Gaslighting and Invalidating

Gaslighting and invalidating are two common toxic behaviors that can be extremely damaging in a relationship. Gaslighting is a form of manipulation where one person makes the other doubt their own reality, memory, or sanity. Invalidating, on the other hand, involves dismissing or minimizing the feelings, experiences, and opinions of the other person. Both of these behaviors can erode a person's self-esteem and sense of self-worth, making it difficult for them to trust their own perceptions and emotions.

Gaslighting is a manipulative tactic that is often used by individuals in toxic relationships to gain power and control over their partner. The term "gaslighting" originated from a play and subsequent movie called "Gas Light," where a husband manipulates his wife into believing she is going insane by dimming the gas lights in their home and then denying that anything has changed when she questions it.
Gaslighting can take many forms and can be subtle or overt. Some common examples of gaslighting include:

1. Denying or minimizing: The gaslighter may deny or downplay events or conversations that have taken place, making the other person question their memory or perception of reality.

2. Blaming and shifting responsibility: Gaslighters often shift blame onto their partner, making them feel guilty or responsible for the problems in the relationship.

3. Withholding information: Gaslighters may intentionally withhold information or keep secrets, leading the other person to doubt their own intuition or instincts.

4. Contradicting and confusing: Gaslighters may contradict themselves or give conflicting information, causing the other person to question their own understanding of the situation.

5. Discrediting and undermining: Gaslighters may undermine the other person's achievements, opinions, or abilities, making them doubt their own

worth and capabilities.

Gaslighting can have severe consequences on the victim's mental health and well-being. It can lead to feelings of confusion, self-doubt, anxiety, and depression. Over time, the victim may lose their sense of self and become completely dependent on the gaslighter for validation and approval.

Invalidating is another toxic behavior that can be equally damaging in a relationship. It involves dismissing or minimizing the feelings, experiences, and opinions of the other person. Invalidating can take various forms, including:

1. Dismissing emotions: Invalidators may belittle or dismiss the other person's emotions, making them feel like their feelings are unimportant or unwarranted.
2. Ignoring or trivializing concerns: Invalidators may ignore or downplay the other person's concerns or problems, making them feel like their issues are insignificant.
3. Mocking or ridiculing: Invalidators may mock or ridicule the other person's thoughts, ideas, or beliefs, making them feel foolish or inadequate.
4. Interrupting or talking over: Invalidators may constantly interrupt or talk over the other person, not allowing them to express themselves fully or be heard.
5. Minimizing achievements: Invalidators may downplay or minimize the other person's achievements or successes, making them feel like their accomplishments are not worthy of recognition.

Invalidating can have a profound impact on a person's self-esteem and self-worth. It can make them question their own emotions, thoughts, and experiences, leading to a loss of confidence and a diminished sense of self.

Both gaslighting and invalidating can have serious consequences on a person's mental and emotional well-being. The constant manipulation, doubt, and dismissal can lead to:

1. Low self-esteem: Gaslighting and invalidating can erode a person's self-esteem, making them doubt their worth and value.
2. Self-doubt: The constant questioning of one's reality and emotions can lead to a loss of trust in oneself and a constant state of self-doubt.
3. Anxiety and depression: Gaslighting and invalidating can contribute to the development of anxiety and depression, as the victim is constantly on edge and feels invalidated in their experiences.
4. Isolation: Gaslighters often isolate their victims from friends and family, making it difficult for them to seek support or validation from others.
5. Loss of identity: Gaslighting and invalidating can cause a person to lose their sense of self and become dependent on the gaslighter for validation and approval.

Recognizing gaslighting and invalidating behaviors is crucial in order to protect oneself from the damaging effects of these toxic behaviors. It is important to trust your instincts and seek support from trusted friends, family, or professionals if you suspect that you are in a toxic relationship. Remember, you deserve to be treated with respect, empathy, and understanding.

CHAPTER 3: UNDERSTANDING CODEPENDENCY

What is Codependency?

Codependency is a term that is often used to describe a dysfunctional pattern of behavior in relationships. It is characterized by an excessive reliance on another person for emotional and psychological needs, often at the expense of one's own well-being. Codependent individuals tend to have a strong desire to please others and have difficulty setting boundaries. They may also have a tendency to enable or rescue others, even when it is not in their best interest.

Codependency can develop in various types of relationships, including romantic partnerships, friendships, and even within families. It often stems from early childhood experiences, such as growing up in a dysfunctional or abusive household. In these environments, individuals may learn to prioritize the needs of others over their own, leading to a pattern of codependent behavior in adulthood.

Recognizing codependent behavior is an essential step in

understanding and addressing codependency in relationships. Here are some common signs of codependent behavior:

1. Low self-esteem: Codependent individuals often have a poor sense of self-worth and rely on others for validation and approval.
2. People-pleasing: Codependent individuals have a strong need to please others and may go to great lengths to gain their acceptance and approval.
3. Difficulty setting boundaries: Codependent individuals struggle to set and enforce healthy boundaries in their relationships. They may fear rejection or abandonment if they assert their own needs and desires.
4. Enabling behavior: Codependent individuals often enable others' unhealthy behaviors by making excuses for them, covering up their mistakes, or taking on their responsibilities.
5. Lack of personal identity: Codependent individuals may have difficulty identifying their own needs, desires, and values. They may define themselves solely through their relationships with others.
6. Fear of abandonment: Codependent individuals often have an intense fear of being alone or abandoned. They may stay in toxic relationships out of fear of being alone or not being able to survive on their own.
7. Difficulty expressing emotions: Codependent individuals may struggle to express their own emotions and may instead focus on the emotions and needs of others.
8. Dependency on others for happiness: Codependent individuals rely on others to fulfill their emotional needs and may feel incomplete or unhappy without a relationship.

Codependency and toxic relationships often go hand in hand.

In a toxic relationship, one or both partners engage in harmful behaviors that undermine the well-being and happiness of the other. Codependent individuals are particularly vulnerable to becoming trapped in toxic relationships due to their strong desire to please others and their difficulty setting boundaries.

In a codependent and toxic relationship, the codependent individual may enable the toxic behavior of their partner, making excuses for their actions or taking on the responsibility for their actions. They may also sacrifice their own needs and well-being to maintain the relationship, even when it is detrimental to their mental and emotional health.

Codependent individuals may also find themselves attracted to toxic partners who exhibit controlling, manipulative, or abusive behaviors. This dynamic reinforces their codependent tendencies and perpetuates the cycle of dysfunction.

Breaking free from codependency is a challenging but necessary step towards healing and establishing healthy relationships. Here are some strategies to help break free from codependency:

1. Self-awareness: Recognize and acknowledge your codependent behaviors and patterns. Understand the underlying reasons for your codependency, such as childhood experiences or low self-esteem.
2. Set boundaries: Learn to set and enforce healthy boundaries in your relationships. Practice saying no and prioritize your own needs and well-being.
3. Develop self-esteem: Work on building your self-esteem and self-worth. Engage in activities that make you feel good about yourself and surround yourself with supportive and positive people.
4. Seek support: Reach out to a therapist or support group specializing in codependency. They can provide guidance, validation, and tools to help you

break free from codependent patterns.

5. Practice self-care: Prioritize self-care activities that nurture your physical, emotional, and mental well-being. This can include exercise, meditation, journaling, or engaging in hobbies that bring you joy.

6. Challenge negative beliefs: Identify and challenge negative beliefs about yourself and relationships. Replace them with positive and empowering beliefs that promote self-love and healthy boundaries.

7. Focus on personal growth: Invest in your personal growth and development. Explore your interests, set goals, and work towards becoming the best version of yourself.

Breaking free from codependency is a journey that requires patience, self-compassion, and a commitment to personal growth. With time and effort, you can break free from codependent patterns and cultivate healthy, fulfilling relationships.

Signs of Codependent Behavior

Codependency is a common issue that can arise in toxic relationships. It is a dysfunctional pattern of behavior where one person excessively relies on another for their emotional needs, often at the expense of their own well-being. Codependent behavior can be subtle and difficult to recognize, but understanding the signs can help you identify if you are in a codependent relationship. Here are some common signs of codependent behavior:

One of the key signs of codependency is a strong desire to please others, often at the expense of your own needs and desires. You may find yourself constantly seeking validation and approval from your partner, going to great lengths to make them happy, even if it means sacrificing your own happiness. This excessive people-pleasing behavior can lead to feelings of resentment and a loss of self-identity.

Codependent individuals often struggle with setting and enforcing healthy boundaries. You may find it challenging to say no to your partner's requests or demands, fearing that it will lead to conflict or rejection. This lack of boundaries can result in a loss of personal autonomy and a blurred sense of self. You may feel responsible for your partner's emotions and actions, taking on their problems as your own.

Codependency is often rooted in low self-esteem and a lack of self-worth. You may have a deep-seated belief that you are not deserving of love and happiness, leading you to seek validation and approval from your partner. This low self-esteem can manifest in seeking external validation, constantly seeking reassurance from your partner, and feeling unworthy of love and affection.

Codependent individuals often have an intense fear of being abandoned or rejected by their partner. This fear can drive you to cling onto the relationship, even if it is toxic and detrimental to your well-being. You may go to great lengths to avoid conflict or disagreement, fearing that it will lead to the end of the relationship. This fear of abandonment can keep you trapped in a cycle of unhealthy behaviors and patterns.

In a codependent relationship, your focus is primarily on meeting your partner's needs, often at the expense of your own. You may neglect your own physical, emotional, and mental well-being in order to prioritize your partner's needs. This self-neglect can lead to feelings of resentment, exhaustion, and a loss of self-identity. It is important to remember that taking care of yourself is not selfish but essential for your overall happiness and well-being.

Codependent individuals often struggle with expressing their own emotions and needs. You may find it challenging to communicate your feelings openly and honestly, fearing that it will lead to conflict or rejection. This difficulty in expressing emotions can result in a buildup of resentment and frustration, as your needs go unmet. It is important to learn healthy communication skills and express your emotions in a constructive and assertive manner.

Codependent individuals often enable their partner's destructive behavior, whether it be addiction, emotional abuse, or other harmful patterns. You may make excuses for your partner's behavior, take on the responsibility for their actions, and try to fix or rescue them from their problems. This enabling behavior can perpetuate the toxic dynamics of the relationship and prevent both parties from seeking the necessary help and support.

Recognizing these signs of codependent behavior is the first step towards healing and breaking free from a toxic relationship. It is important to remember that codependency is not a healthy or sustainable way to engage in a relationship. Seeking professional help and support can provide you with the tools and guidance needed to overcome codependency and establish healthy boundaries in your relationships.

———

Codependency in Toxic Relationships

Codependency is a common dynamic that can often be found in toxic relationships. It is a dysfunctional pattern of behavior where one person becomes excessively reliant on another for their sense of self-worth, validation, and emotional well-being. In a codependent relationship, there is an unhealthy imbalance of power and control, with one person taking on the role of the caretaker or enabler, while the other person becomes dependent and manipulative.

Codependency is rooted in deep-seated emotional issues and often stems from childhood experiences. It can develop when a person grows up in a dysfunctional family environment, where their emotional needs were not met, and they were forced to take on adult responsibilities at a young age. This can lead to a distorted sense of self and a belief that their worth is dependent on taking care of others.

In a codependent relationship, the codependent individual often sacrifices their own needs and desires to meet the needs of their partner. They may have a strong fear of abandonment and will go to great lengths to avoid conflict or disapproval. This can result in a loss of personal identity and a lack of boundaries, as the codependent individual becomes enmeshed with their partner's emotions and behaviors.

Recognizing codependent behavior is crucial in understanding the dynamics of a toxic relationship. Here are some common signs of codependency:

1. Low self-esteem: Codependent individuals often have a poor sense of self-worth and rely on external validation to feel good about themselves.
2. People-pleasing: Codependents have a strong need to please others, often at the expense of their own well-being. They may struggle to say no and fear rejection or disapproval.
3. Difficulty setting boundaries: Codependents have a hard time establishing and enforcing boundaries. They may feel guilty or anxious when asserting their needs or saying no to others.
4. Enabling behavior: Codependents often enable their partner's unhealthy behaviors, such as addiction or abusive tendencies, in an attempt to maintain the

relationship or avoid conflict.

5. Lack of personal identity: Codependents may have a weak sense of self and struggle to identify their own wants, needs, and desires separate from their partner's.

6. Fear of abandonment: Codependents have an intense fear of being alone or abandoned, which can lead them to stay in toxic relationships even when they are unhappy or mistreated.

7. Difficulty expressing emotions: Codependents may struggle to express their own emotions and needs, as they have become accustomed to prioritizing their partner's emotions and needs.

Codependency often goes hand in hand with toxic relationships. In a toxic relationship, one partner may exhibit controlling, manipulative, or abusive behaviors, while the other partner becomes codependent and enables these behaviors. The codependent individual may believe that they can change or fix their partner, and they may take on the responsibility for their partner's happiness and well-being.

In a codependent toxic relationship, the codependent individual may ignore or dismiss their own needs and boundaries to maintain the relationship. They may make excuses for their partner's behavior, blame themselves for the problems in the relationship, and feel a sense of guilt or shame when they consider leaving.

The toxic partner may exploit the codependent's need for validation and control, using manipulation, gaslighting, or emotional abuse to maintain power and control over the relationship. This creates a cycle of dependency, where the codependent individual becomes increasingly reliant on their partner for their sense of self-worth and validation.

Breaking free from codependency is essential for healing from a toxic relationship and establishing healthy boundaries. Here are some steps to break free from codependency:

1. Self-awareness: Recognize and acknowledge the codependent patterns in your behavior and the impact they have on your well-being.
2. Educate yourself: Learn about codependency and its underlying causes. Understanding the roots of codependency can help you gain insight into your own behavior and make positive changes.
3. Therapy and support: Seek therapy or counseling to address the underlying emotional issues that contribute to codependency. A therapist can provide guidance, support, and tools to help you break free from codependent patterns.
4. Develop self-care practices: Prioritize self-care and self-compassion. Engage in activities that bring you joy, practice self-care rituals, and cultivate a strong sense of self-worth.
5. Set and enforce boundaries: Learn to establish and enforce healthy boundaries in your relationships. Communicate your needs and desires clearly and assertively, and be willing to say no when necessary.
6. Build a support system: Surround yourself with supportive and understanding individuals who can provide encouragement and validation as you navigate your journey towards healing.
7. Practice self-reflection: Continuously reflect on your thoughts, feelings, and behaviors. Be mindful of any codependent tendencies and make a conscious effort to make choices that align with your own well-being.

Breaking free from codependency takes time and effort, but it is a crucial step towards healing and creating healthier relationships in the future. Remember, you deserve to be in a relationship that is based on mutual respect, trust, and support.

——

Breaking Free from Codependency

Toxic relationships can be incredibly damaging to our mental and emotional well-being. They can drain our energy, erode our self-esteem, and prevent us from living a fulfilling life. Recognizing a toxic relationship is the first step towards breaking free from its grip. Here are some signs to look out for:

1. Lack of respect: In a toxic relationship, there is a lack of respect for each other's boundaries, opinions, and feelings. Disrespectful behavior can manifest as belittling, name-calling, or constant criticism.

2. Control and manipulation: Toxic partners often use control and manipulation tactics to maintain power and dominance. They may try to control your actions, isolate you from friends and family, or make decisions without your input.

3. Constant criticism: In a toxic relationship, criticism becomes a regular occurrence. Your partner may constantly find fault with your appearance, abilities, or choices, leaving you feeling inadequate and insecure.

4. Emotional abuse: Emotional abuse can take many forms, including gaslighting, guilt-tripping, and emotional blackmail. Your partner may manipulate your emotions to make you doubt yourself or feel responsible for their actions.

5. Lack of trust: Trust is the foundation of any healthy relationship. In a toxic relationship, trust is often broken through lies, deceit, or infidelity. Constant suspicion and jealousy can also indicate a lack of trust.

6. Unbalanced power dynamics: Toxic relationships often have imbalanced power dynamics, with one

partner exerting control and dominance over the other. This can lead to feelings of powerlessness and a loss of autonomy.

7. Constant conflict: While conflict is a normal part of any relationship, toxic relationships are characterized by constant and unresolved conflict. Arguments may escalate quickly, and there may be a pattern of blame-shifting and refusal to take responsibility.

8. Emotional and physical exhaustion: Toxic relationships can be emotionally and physically draining. Constant stress, anxiety, and feelings of being on edge can leave you feeling exhausted and depleted.

9. Isolation from support systems: Toxic partners often try to isolate their victims from friends and family. They may discourage or prevent you from spending time with loved ones, leaving you feeling isolated and dependent on them.

10. Lack of reciprocity: Healthy relationships are built on mutual respect, support, and reciprocity. In a toxic relationship, one partner may consistently prioritize their own needs and desires, neglecting the needs of the other person.

It's important to remember that no relationship is perfect, and occasional disagreements or conflicts are normal. However, if these signs are consistently present in your relationship, it may be time to evaluate whether it is toxic and unhealthy.

Recognizing a toxic relationship is the first step towards breaking free and reclaiming your life. It's essential to prioritize your well-being and seek support from trusted friends, family, or professionals. Remember, you deserve to be in a loving and healthy relationship.

CHAPTER 4: EXPLORING UNHEALTHY RELATIONSHIP PATTERNS

Repeating Patterns from Childhood

Childhood experiences play a significant role in shaping our beliefs, behaviors, and patterns in adulthood. When it comes to relationships, the patterns we witnessed or experienced during our formative years can have a profound impact on the types of relationships we seek out and engage in. In this section, we will explore the concept of repeating patterns from childhood and how they can contribute to

Repeating patterns refer to the tendency to recreate familiar dynamics and behaviors from our past in our present relationships. These patterns can stem from various sources, including our family of origin, early experiences, and the relationships we observed growing up. They often manifest as unconscious behaviors and beliefs that we carry with us into adulthood.

Our family of origin, which includes our parents or primary caregivers, siblings, and other family members, serves as our first model for relationships. The dynamics and interactions we witnessed within our family unit can shape our understanding of what is considered normal or acceptable in relationships. If we grew up in an environment where toxic behaviors were prevalent, such as emotional or physical abuse, neglect, or constant conflict, we may unknowingly seek out similar dynamics in our adult relationships.

Unresolved childhood trauma can also contribute to the repetition of unhealthy relationship patterns. Traumatic experiences, such as abuse, abandonment, or loss, can leave deep emotional wounds that impact our ability to form healthy connections with others. Without proper healing and support, these unresolved traumas can manifest in our adult relationships, leading to patterns of codependency, emotional unavailability, or even abusive behaviors.

The beliefs and messages we internalize during childhood can significantly influence our relationship patterns. If we grew up in an environment where we were constantly criticized, belittled, or made to feel unworthy, we may develop low self-esteem and a belief that we do not deserve healthy, loving relationships. As a result, we may find ourselves gravitating towards toxic relationships that reinforce these negative beliefs about ourselves.

Human beings are creatures of habit, and we often seek out what is familiar and comfortable, even if it is unhealthy. This tendency to gravitate towards what we know can lead us to unconsciously recreate the same dynamics and patterns we experienced in our childhood. We may find ourselves drawn to partners who exhibit similar traits or behaviors as our parents or caregivers, even if those traits are toxic or harmful.

Recognizing and breaking free from repeating patterns from childhood is essential for breaking the cycle of unhealthy relationships. Here are some steps you can take to begin this process:

1. Self-reflection: Take the time to reflect on your past and the relationships you witnessed or experienced during your childhood. Consider the dynamics, behaviors, and beliefs that were present and how they may be influencing your current relationships.

2. Therapy or counseling: Seeking professional help can provide valuable insights and support in understanding and healing from childhood trauma and unhealthy relationship patterns. A therapist can help you explore your past, identify patterns, and develop healthier coping mechanisms.

3. Self-awareness: Cultivate self-awareness by paying attention to your thoughts, emotions, and behaviors in your relationships. Notice any recurring patterns or triggers that may be rooted in your childhood experiences.

4. Healing and self-care: Prioritize your healing and self-care. Engage in activities that promote self-love, self-compassion, and emotional well-being. This may include practicing mindfulness, engaging in hobbies, seeking support from loved ones, or participating in therapy or support groups.

5. Setting boundaries: Establishing and enforcing healthy boundaries is crucial in breaking free from repeating patterns. Learn to identify and communicate your needs and limits in relationships, and surround yourself with people who respect and support your boundaries.

Remember, breaking free from repeating patterns from

childhood takes time and effort. Be patient with yourself and seek support when needed. By recognizing and addressing these patterns, you can create healthier and more fulfilling relationships in your life.

———

Enabling and Enmeshment

Enabling and enmeshment are two unhealthy relationship patterns that can contribute to the toxicity of a relationship. These patterns often go hand in hand and can be difficult to recognize, as they may initially appear to be acts of love and support. However, over time, enabling and enmeshment can lead to codependency and a loss of individuality within the relationship.

Enabling is a behavior in which one person consistently supports and enables the unhealthy actions or behaviors of their partner. This can include making excuses for their partner's actions, covering up their mistakes, or taking on responsibilities that should be their partner's. Enablers often have good intentions and believe that they are helping their partner, but in reality, they are preventing their partner from taking responsibility for their actions and facing the consequences.

Enabling can manifest in various ways within a toxic relationship. For example, if one partner is struggling with addiction, the other partner may enable their behavior by providing them with drugs or alcohol, or by making excuses for their behavior to others. In another scenario, if one partner is emotionally abusive, the other partner may enable their behavior by accepting the blame for their actions or by constantly trying to please them in order to avoid conflict.

Enabling can be damaging to both individuals in the relationship. The enabler may become emotionally drained and lose their sense of self, as they are constantly focused on meeting the needs of their partner. The person being enabled may never face the consequences of their actions, which can hinder their personal growth and perpetuate their unhealthy behaviors.

Enmeshment is a pattern in which boundaries between individuals in a relationship become blurred or nonexistent. In an enmeshed relationship, there is a lack of individuality and personal autonomy, as the boundaries between partners are crossed and personal identities become intertwined. This can lead to a loss of self and a sense of being controlled or suffocated within the relationship.

Enmeshment often occurs when there is a lack of healthy boundaries within a relationship. This can be due to a variety of factors, such as a history of trauma, a fear of abandonment, or a desire for constant closeness and validation. In an enmeshed relationship, partners may have difficulty making decisions independently, as they are constantly seeking approval or validation from their partner. They may also struggle with maintaining separate identities and may feel a sense of anxiety or guilt when pursuing individual interests or spending time apart.

Enmeshment can be detrimental to both individuals in the relationship. It can hinder personal growth and development, as individuals may struggle to establish their own identities and pursue their own goals and interests. It can also lead to a lack of healthy communication and conflict resolution, as partners may avoid expressing their true thoughts and feelings in order to maintain the illusion of harmony within the relationship.

Recognizing and breaking the patterns of enabling and enmeshment is crucial for healing from a toxic relationship. Here are some steps you can take to break free from these unhealthy patterns:

1. Self-awareness: Take the time to reflect on your own behaviors and patterns within the relationship. Recognize if you have been enabling your partner's unhealthy actions or if you have become enmeshed in the relationship.
2. Set boundaries: Establish clear boundaries within the relationship and communicate them to your partner. This includes defining what behaviors are acceptable and what behaviors are not. Stick to these boundaries and hold your partner accountable for their actions.
3. Seek support: Reach out to trusted friends, family members, or a therapist who can provide guidance and support as you navigate the process of breaking free from enabling and enmeshment. They can offer an outside perspective and help you stay accountable to your boundaries.
4. Focus on self-care: Prioritize your own well-being and self-care. Engage in activities that bring you joy and fulfillment, and take time to nurture your own personal growth and development.
5. Seek professional help: If the patterns of enabling and enmeshment are deeply ingrained and difficult to break on your own, consider seeking the help of a therapist or counselor who specializes in toxic relationships. They can provide you with the tools and strategies to overcome these patterns and build healthier relationship dynamics.

Breaking free from the patterns of enabling and enmeshment takes time and effort, but it is essential for your own personal growth and well-being. By recognizing these patterns and taking steps to establish healthy boundaries, you can create a more balanced and fulfilling relationship moving forward.

———

Cycle of Abuse

In toxic relationships, there is often a recurring pattern of abusive behavior known as the cycle of abuse. This cycle consists of four distinct phases: tension building, explosion, reconciliation, and calm. Understanding this cycle is crucial for recognizing and addressing toxic relationships.

The first phase of the cycle of abuse is tension building. During this phase, there is a gradual increase in tension and conflict within the relationship. Small disagreements and arguments may occur more frequently, and communication becomes strained. The victim may feel a sense of walking on eggshells, constantly trying to avoid triggering the abuser's anger or aggression.

In this phase, the abuser may display signs of irritability, criticism, and controlling behavior. They may become increasingly demanding, possessive, or jealous. The victim may try to appease the abuser, believing that their efforts will prevent the situation from escalating further.

The tension building phase eventually leads to the explosion phase. This is when the abusive behavior reaches its peak, resulting in verbal, emotional, physical, or sexual abuse. The explosion phase is characterized by intense outbursts of anger, aggression, and violence.

During this phase, the victim may experience physical harm, emotional trauma, or both. The abuser may use various tactics to exert power and control, such as physical violence, threats, intimidation, or manipulation. The victim may feel helpless, frightened, and trapped in the abusive relationship.

After the explosion phase, the cycle of abuse enters the reconciliation phase. In this phase, the abuser may show remorse, apologize, and make promises to change their behavior. They may express love, affection, and kindness towards the victim, creating a temporary sense of relief and hope.

During this phase, the victim may feel conflicted and confused. They may want to believe that the abuser will change and that the relationship can improve. The abuser may use this opportunity to manipulate the victim into staying in the relationship, promising that things will be different in the future.

The final phase of the cycle of abuse is the calm phase. During this phase, the tension and conflict temporarily subside, and the relationship appears to be peaceful. The abuser may act loving, attentive, and supportive, creating a false sense of security for the victim.

In this phase, the victim may feel relieved and hopeful that the abusive behavior has ended. They may convince themselves that the relationship is improving and that the abuser has changed. However, this calm phase is only temporary, and the cycle of abuse will eventually restart with the tension building phase.

Recognizing the cycle of abuse is essential for breaking free from a toxic relationship. It is important to understand that the cycle will continue unless intervention and change occur. Here are some steps to break the cycle of abuse:

1. Educate Yourself: Learn about the dynamics of toxic relationships and the cycle of abuse. Understanding the patterns and behaviors involved will help you recognize and address them.
2. Seek Support: Reach out to trusted friends, family members, or support groups who can provide emotional support and guidance. They can help you gain perspective and offer assistance in breaking free

from the toxic relationship.

3. Safety Planning: If you are in immediate danger, create a safety plan to protect yourself. This may involve finding a safe place to stay, contacting local authorities, or seeking assistance from domestic violence organizations.

4. Establish Boundaries: Set clear boundaries with the abuser and communicate your expectations for respectful behavior. Enforce these boundaries and seek professional help if they are repeatedly violated.

5. Seek Professional Help: Consider seeking therapy or counseling to address the emotional and psychological impact of the abusive relationship. A trained professional can provide guidance, support, and tools for healing and recovery.

6. Develop a Support System: Surround yourself with a network of supportive individuals who can provide encouragement, validation, and assistance throughout your healing journey. This may include friends, family, therapists, or support groups.

7. Focus on Self-Care: Prioritize self-care and engage in activities that promote your physical, emotional, and mental well-being. Practice self-compassion, engage in hobbies, and take time for relaxation and self-reflection.

Breaking the cycle of abuse requires courage, support, and a commitment to your own well-being. Remember that you deserve to be in a healthy and loving relationship. By recognizing the cycle of abuse and taking steps to break free, you can begin the journey towards healing and creating a life free from toxicity.

———

Toxic Communication Patterns

Toxic communication patterns are a common characteristic of unhealthy relationships. These patterns can be subtle or overt, but they all have one thing in common: they erode the foundation of trust and respect between partners. In this section, we will explore some of the most common toxic communication patterns and provide guidance on how to recognize and address them.

Passive-aggressive behavior is a toxic communication pattern that involves expressing negative feelings indirectly or through subtle actions. It can manifest as sarcasm, backhanded compliments, or intentionally withholding information. This behavior is often driven by a fear of confrontation or a desire to maintain control over the relationship.

Recognizing passive-aggressive behavior can be challenging because it is often disguised as humor or innocent remarks. However, if you find yourself frequently feeling hurt or confused by your partner's comments or actions, it may be a sign of passive-aggressive behavior. Pay attention to the underlying tone and intention behind their words and actions.

To address passive-aggressive behavior, it is important to communicate openly and honestly with your partner. Express your feelings and concerns in a calm and non-confrontational manner. Encourage them to do the same and work together to find healthier ways to express emotions and resolve conflicts.

Stonewalling is a toxic communication pattern characterized by withdrawing from a conversation or shutting down emotionally. It often occurs when one partner feels overwhelmed or unable to handle conflict. Stonewalling can leave the other partner feeling ignored, dismissed, and frustrated.

Recognizing stonewalling can be challenging because it can be mistaken for someone needing space or time to process their emotions. However, if your partner consistently avoids or refuses to engage in important conversations, it may be a sign of stonewalling. Look for patterns of emotional withdrawal, silence, or disengagement during discussions.

To address stonewalling, it is important to create a safe and non-judgmental space for open communication. Encourage your partner to express their feelings and concerns without fear of judgment or criticism. Seek professional help if necessary to learn effective communication strategies and rebuild trust and emotional connection.

Blaming and defensiveness are toxic communication patterns that often go hand in hand. Blaming involves holding the other person responsible for problems or conflicts, while defensiveness involves denying responsibility and shifting blame onto the other person. These patterns can create a cycle of negativity and prevent effective problem-solving.

Recognizing blaming and defensiveness can be challenging because they can be subtle and ingrained in the dynamics of the relationship. However, if you find yourself constantly being blamed for issues or if your partner consistently avoids taking responsibility for their actions, it may be a sign of these toxic communication patterns.

To address blaming and defensiveness, it is important to foster a culture of accountability and empathy in the relationship. Encourage open and honest communication where both partners take responsibility for their actions and work together to find solutions. Practice active listening and validate each other's feelings to create a safe and supportive environment.

Invalidating and dismissive behavior is a toxic communication pattern that involves minimizing or disregarding the other person's feelings, experiences, or opinions. It can manifest as belittling, mocking, or ignoring the other person's perspective.

This pattern can erode self-esteem and create a sense of worthlessness in the relationship.

Recognizing invalidating and dismissive behavior can be challenging because it can be subtle and disguised as jokes or harmless comments. However, if you consistently feel invalidated or dismissed by your partner, it may be a sign of this toxic communication pattern. Pay attention to how your partner responds to your emotions and opinions.

To address invalidating and dismissive behavior, it is important to establish clear boundaries and communicate your needs assertively. Express how their behavior makes you feel and request that they validate and respect your emotions and opinions. Seek couples therapy or individual counseling if necessary to address underlying issues and improve communication skills.

Recognizing and addressing toxic communication patterns is essential for creating a healthier and more fulfilling relationship. By understanding these patterns and taking proactive steps to address them, you can foster open and respectful communication that strengthens the bond between you and your partner.

CHAPTER 5: THE IMPACT OF TOXIC RELATIONSHIPS ON SELF-ESTEEM

Understanding Self-Esteem

Self-esteem is a fundamental aspect of our overall well-being and mental health. It refers to how we perceive and value ourselves, our beliefs about our worthiness, and our ability to love and accept ourselves. Self-esteem plays a crucial role in our relationships, as it influences how we interact with others and how we allow others to treat us.

Having a healthy level of self-esteem is essential for our emotional and psychological well-being. When we have high self-esteem, we have a positive self-image, believe in our abilities, and have confidence in our decisions. This positive self-perception allows us to set healthy boundaries, make choices that align with our values, and engage in fulfilling relationships.

On the other hand, low self-esteem can have detrimental effects on our lives, particularly in the context of toxic relationships. When we have low self-esteem, we may doubt our worth, constantly seek validation from others, and tolerate mistreatment. This can lead us to stay in toxic relationships, as we may believe that we don't deserve better or fear being alone.

Toxic relationships can have a profound impact on our self-esteem, often causing it to deteriorate over time. In a toxic relationship, the dynamics are characterized by manipulation, control, and emotional abuse. These behaviors can chip away at our self-worth and confidence, leaving us feeling powerless and unworthy of love and respect.

One of the ways toxic relationships affect self-esteem is through constant criticism and belittlement. Toxic partners may engage in name-calling, insults, and demeaning comments, which can erode our self-image and make us question our worth. Over time, we may internalize these negative messages and start to believe that we are indeed inadequate or unworthy.

Another way toxic relationships impact self-esteem is through gaslighting. Gaslighting is a manipulative tactic used by toxic individuals to make their partners doubt their own perceptions and reality. They may deny or distort events, manipulate facts, and make their partners question their sanity. Gaslighting can leave us feeling confused, doubting our own judgment, and ultimately eroding our self-trust and self-esteem.

Additionally, toxic relationships often involve control and manipulation. Toxic partners may exert control over various aspects of our lives, such as our friendships, finances, or career choices. This constant control can make us feel powerless and diminish our sense of autonomy and self-worth. We may start to doubt our abilities to make decisions and become dependent on the toxic partner for validation and approval.

Rebuilding self-esteem after a toxic relationship is a process that takes time, patience, and self-compassion. Here are some strategies to help you regain your self-worth and rebuild your self-esteem:

1. Practice self-care: Engage in activities that nourish your mind, body, and soul. Take care of your physical health, engage in hobbies you enjoy, and prioritize self-care practices such as meditation, journaling, or spending time in nature. Taking care of yourself sends a powerful message that you value and deserve love and care.

2. Challenge negative self-talk: Pay attention to your inner dialogue and challenge negative thoughts and beliefs about yourself. Replace self-critical thoughts with positive affirmations and remind yourself of your strengths and accomplishments. Surround yourself with supportive and positive people who uplift and encourage you.

3. Set boundaries: Establishing and enforcing healthy boundaries is crucial for rebuilding self-esteem. Clearly define what is acceptable and unacceptable behavior in your relationships and communicate your boundaries assertively. Learning to say no and prioritize your needs sends a message that you value and respect yourself.

4. Seek support: Reach out to trusted friends, family members, or a therapist who can provide emotional support and guidance. Talking about your experiences and feelings with someone who understands can help you process your emotions and gain perspective on the toxic relationship.

5. Focus on personal growth: Engage in activities that promote personal growth and self-improvement. Set goals for yourself and work towards achieving them. This can help you regain a sense of purpose and accomplishment, boosting your self-esteem in the process.

6. Practice self-compassion: Be kind and gentle with yourself as you navigate the healing process. Understand that healing takes time and that setbacks are a normal part of the journey. Treat yourself with the same compassion and understanding you would offer to a dear friend.

Remember, rebuilding self-esteem is a gradual process, and it's important to be patient and kind to yourself along the way. Surround yourself with positive influences, engage in self-care, and seek support when needed. With time and effort, you can rebuild your self-esteem and create a healthier, more fulfilling life for yourself.

——

How Toxic Relationships Affect Self-Esteem

Toxic relationships can have a profound impact on an individual's self-esteem. When we are in a toxic relationship, our self-worth and confidence can be slowly eroded over time. The negative behaviors and dynamics within the relationship can leave us feeling unworthy, unlovable, and powerless. Understanding how toxic relationships affect self-esteem is crucial in recognizing the need for change and taking steps towards healing and rebuilding.

One of the ways toxic relationships affect self-esteem is through the cycle of emotional abuse. Emotional abuse involves the consistent use of manipulative tactics, such as belittling, criticizing, and demeaning the other person. This constant emotional assault can lead to feelings of worthlessness and self-doubt. The victim may start to internalize the negative messages and believe that they are indeed unworthy of love and respect.

Gaslighting is another toxic behavior that can severely impact self-esteem. Gaslighting involves manipulating someone into questioning their own reality and sanity. The gaslighter may deny or distort the truth, making the victim doubt their own perceptions and experiences. This constant invalidation can lead to a loss of self-trust and confidence. The victim may start to question their own judgment and feel like they are going crazy, further damaging their self-esteem.

In a toxic relationship, constant criticism and negativity can wear down a person's self-esteem. When someone is constantly criticized, their self-worth is undermined, and they may start to believe that they are inherently flawed or inadequate. The negative comments and constant put-downs can create a negative self-image and erode any sense of self-confidence.

Toxic relationships often involve isolating the victim from their support system and creating a sense of dependency. The toxic partner may discourage or prevent the victim from spending time with friends and family, making them feel isolated and alone. This isolation can further damage self-esteem as the victim may start to believe that they are unworthy of healthy relationships and support. The dependency created by the toxic partner can also make the victim feel powerless and incapable of making decisions on their own, further eroding their self-esteem.

Toxic relationships are often characterized by manipulation and control. The toxic partner may use various tactics to control the other person's thoughts, emotions, and actions. This constant manipulation can make the victim feel powerless and incapable of making their own choices. The loss of autonomy and agency can have a detrimental effect on self-esteem, as the victim may start to doubt their own abilities and feel like they have no control over their own life.

Being in a toxic relationship can be emotionally and physically exhausting. The constant stress, conflict, and turmoil can drain a person's energy and leave them feeling depleted. This exhaustion can further impact self-esteem, as the individual may struggle to find the motivation and energy to take care of themselves and pursue their own goals and interests. The constant state of exhaustion can also make it difficult for the victim to see a way out of the toxic relationship, further damaging their self-esteem.

In toxic relationships, the toxic partner often shifts the blame onto the victim, making them feel responsible for the problems in the relationship. The victim may internalize this blame and feel guilty for the toxic dynamics. This internalized guilt can lead to feelings of shame and further damage self-esteem. The victim may start to believe that they are the cause of the toxicity and that they deserve the mistreatment, further eroding their self-worth.

Toxic relationships can also result in a loss of identity. The toxic partner may try to control and mold the other person into someone they want them to be, rather than accepting them for who they are. This loss of individuality and authenticity can have a significant impact on self-esteem. The victim may start to question their own worth and value, as they are constantly being told that they are not good enough as they are.

Toxic relationships can have a profound and detrimental effect on an individual's self-esteem. The cycle of emotional abuse, gaslighting, constant criticism, isolation, manipulation, and control can all contribute to a loss of self-worth and confidence. Recognizing the impact of toxic relationships on self-esteem is the first step towards healing and rebuilding. It is essential to seek support, set boundaries, and prioritize self-care in order to regain a healthy sense of self and move towards thriving in life.

———

Rebuilding Self-Esteem After

a Toxic Relationship

Rebuilding self-esteem after a toxic relationship is a crucial step towards healing and moving forward. Toxic relationships can have a significant impact on our self-worth and confidence, leaving us feeling broken and depleted. However, with time, self-reflection, and self-care, it is possible to rebuild and regain a healthy sense of self-esteem.

The first step in rebuilding self-esteem after a toxic relationship is to acknowledge and accept your feelings. It is normal to feel hurt, betrayed, and even ashamed after being in a toxic relationship. Allow yourself to feel these emotions without judgment or self-blame. Recognize that your feelings are valid and that it is okay to grieve the loss of the relationship.

Self-compassion is a vital component of rebuilding self-esteem. Treat yourself with kindness, understanding, and forgiveness. Remind yourself that you deserve love and respect. Practice self-compassion by engaging in positive self-talk, challenging negative beliefs, and embracing self-care activities that nourish your mind, body, and soul.

Toxic relationships often leave us with negative beliefs about ourselves. These beliefs can manifest as negative self-talk, where we constantly criticize and belittle ourselves. Challenge these negative thoughts by questioning their validity and replacing them with positive affirmations. Surround yourself with supportive and uplifting people who can help counteract the negative self-talk.

Setting realistic goals and celebrating your achievements is an effective way to rebuild self-esteem. Start small and focus on achievable goals that align with your values and interests. As you accomplish these goals, celebrate your achievements and acknowledge your progress. This will help boost your self-confidence and reinforce a positive self-image.

Self-reflection is a powerful tool for rebuilding self-esteem. Take the time to reflect on the toxic relationship and identify any patterns or behaviors that contributed to it. This self-awareness will help you grow and make healthier choices in future relationships. Engage in personal growth activities such as therapy, journaling, or self-help books to deepen your understanding of yourself and build resilience.

Building a strong support system is essential for rebuilding self-esteem. Surround yourself with friends, family, or support groups who uplift and validate your experiences. Seek out individuals who genuinely care about your well-being and can provide a safe space for you to heal. Avoid people who undermine your progress or try to bring you back into toxic dynamics.

Self-care is a crucial aspect of rebuilding self-esteem. Prioritize your physical, emotional, and mental well-being by engaging in activities that bring you joy and relaxation. This can include exercise, meditation, hobbies, or spending time in nature. Nourish your body with nutritious food, get enough sleep, and practice self-care rituals that make you feel good about yourself.

Rebuilding self-esteem involves setting healthy boundaries and prioritizing your needs. Learn to assertively communicate your boundaries and say no to things that do not align with your values or well-being. Prioritize self-care and make time for activities that bring you happiness and fulfillment. By setting boundaries and prioritizing your needs, you are sending a message to yourself and others that you deserve respect and love.

Rebuilding self-esteem after a toxic relationship can be challenging, and it is okay to seek professional help if needed. A therapist or counselor can provide guidance, support, and tools to help you navigate the healing process. They can assist you in uncovering underlying issues, developing coping strategies, and rebuilding your self-esteem in a healthy and sustainable way.

Practicing gratitude and positive affirmations can significantly impact your self-esteem. Take time each day to reflect on the things you are grateful for, no matter how small. This will shift your focus from negativity to positivity and help you appreciate your worth. Additionally, repeat positive affirmations that reinforce your self-worth and remind yourself of your strengths and capabilities.

Rebuilding self-esteem after a toxic relationship requires embracing forgiveness and letting go. Forgive yourself for any perceived mistakes or shortcomings and let go of any resentment or anger towards your ex-partner. Holding onto negative emotions only hinders your healing process. By forgiving and letting go, you free yourself from the burden of the past and create space for self-growth and self-love.

Rebuilding self-esteem involves embracing your individuality and exploring your passions. Take the time to rediscover who you are outside of the toxic relationship. Engage in activities that bring you joy and allow you to express your authentic self. Embrace your unique qualities and celebrate your strengths. By embracing your individuality and pursuing your passions, you will cultivate a strong sense of self-esteem and fulfillment.

Rebuilding self-esteem after a toxic relationship is a journey that requires patience, self-compassion, and self-reflection. Remember that healing takes time, and it is okay to seek support along the way. By prioritizing your well-being, setting boundaries, and engaging in self-care, you can rebuild your self-esteem and create a healthier and happier future for yourself.

——

Self-Care and Self-Compassion

Self-care and self-compassion are essential components of healing and recovering from a toxic relationship. When you have been in a toxic relationship, it is common to feel depleted, emotionally drained, and have a diminished sense of self-worth. Engaging in self-care practices and cultivating self-compassion can help you rebuild your self-esteem, regain your sense of self, and create a foundation for a healthier future.

Self-care involves intentionally taking care of your physical, emotional, and mental well-being. It is about recognizing your needs and making a conscious effort to meet them. In the aftermath of a toxic relationship, self-care becomes even more crucial as you work towards healing and rebuilding your life. Here are some self-care practices that can support your healing journey:

1. Physical self-care: Take care of your body by engaging in activities that promote physical well-being. This can include regular exercise, getting enough sleep, eating nutritious meals, and practicing relaxation techniques such as yoga or meditation.

2. Emotional self-care: Allow yourself to feel and process your emotions. Give yourself permission to grieve the loss of the relationship and acknowledge any pain or hurt you may be experiencing. Seek support from trusted friends, family, or a therapist who can provide a safe space for you to express your emotions.

3. Mental self-care: Engage in activities that stimulate your mind and promote mental well-being. This can include reading books, learning new skills, engaging in creative outlets such as painting or writing, or practicing mindfulness and meditation to cultivate a sense of calm and clarity.

4. Social self-care: Surround yourself with supportive

and positive people who uplift and encourage you. Seek out healthy relationships and connections that nourish your soul. Engage in activities that bring you joy and allow you to connect with others who share similar interests.

5. Spiritual self-care: Explore and nurture your spiritual beliefs and practices. This can involve engaging in prayer, meditation, or attending religious or spiritual gatherings that align with your beliefs. Connecting with your spirituality can provide a sense of purpose, meaning, and inner peace.

Remember, self-care is not selfish. It is a necessary act of self-preservation and self-love. By prioritizing your well-being, you are better equipped to heal from the wounds of a toxic relationship and create a healthier and happier life.

Self-compassion is the practice of treating yourself with kindness, understanding, and acceptance, especially during challenging times. It involves extending the same compassion and empathy towards yourself that you would offer to a dear friend or loved one. Cultivating self-compassion is crucial in the healing process after a toxic relationship.

Here are some ways to cultivate self-compassion:

1. Practice self-kindness: Be gentle and understanding with yourself. Treat yourself with the same kindness and compassion you would show to someone you care about. Acknowledge your pain and struggles without judgment or self-criticism.

2. Validate your emotions: Allow yourself to feel and validate your emotions without judgment. Recognize that it is normal to experience a range of emotions after a toxic relationship, including anger, sadness, and confusion. Give yourself permission to process

these emotions and seek support when needed.

3. Challenge self-judgment: Notice and challenge any self-critical thoughts or beliefs that may arise. Replace self-judgment with self-compassionate statements. Remind yourself that you are deserving of love, understanding, and forgiveness.

4. Practice mindfulness: Cultivate present-moment awareness and non-judgmental acceptance of your thoughts and emotions. Mindfulness can help you observe your experiences without getting caught up in self-critical or negative thought patterns.

5. Seek support: Reach out to trusted friends, family, or a therapist who can provide support and guidance on your healing journey. Surrounding yourself with compassionate and understanding individuals can help reinforce self-compassion and provide a safe space for you to process your emotions.

Remember, healing takes time, and it is essential to be patient and gentle with yourself throughout the process. By practicing self-care and self-compassion, you are taking active steps towards reclaiming your self-worth and creating a life filled with love, joy, and fulfillment.

CHAPTER 6: HEALING FROM A TOXIC RELATIONSHIP

Recognizing the Need for Healing

Recognizing the need for healing is the first step towards breaking free from a toxic relationship. It can be a difficult and painful process, but it is essential for your well-being and personal growth. In this section, we will explore the signs that indicate you are in a toxic relationship and the importance of acknowledging the need for healing.

To recognize the need for healing, it is crucial to understand the signs of a toxic relationship. Here are some common indicators that you may be in a toxic relationship:

1. Constant criticism and belittling: If your partner consistently puts you down, criticizes your every move, and makes you feel worthless, it is a clear sign of a toxic relationship.

2. Lack of respect and boundaries: In a healthy relationship, both partners respect each other's boundaries. However, in a toxic relationship,

boundaries are often disregarded, and one partner may try to control or manipulate the other.

3. Emotional manipulation: Manipulation is a key characteristic of toxic relationships. Your partner may use guilt, fear, or other tactics to control your actions and emotions.

4. Isolation from friends and family: Toxic partners often try to isolate their victims from their support system. They may discourage you from spending time with friends and family or make you feel guilty for doing so.

5. Constant conflict and volatility: Toxic relationships are characterized by frequent arguments, yelling, and emotional outbursts. The relationship may feel like a rollercoaster ride, with extreme highs and lows.

6. Lack of trust and honesty: Trust is the foundation of any healthy relationship. In a toxic relationship, trust is often broken, and there is a lack of honesty and transparency.

7. Feeling drained and exhausted: Toxic relationships can be emotionally and physically draining. If you constantly feel exhausted, anxious, or depressed when you are with your partner, it may be a sign that the relationship is toxic.

8. Feeling trapped and powerless: Toxic relationships often make you feel trapped and powerless. You may feel like you have no control over your own life and decisions.

9. Cycle of abuse: If you find yourself in a repetitive cycle of abuse, where your partner apologizes and promises to change, only to repeat the same harmful behaviors, it is a clear sign of a toxic relationship.

10. Lack of support and empathy: In a healthy relationship, both partners support and empathize with each other. However, in a toxic relationship, your partner may lack empathy and dismiss your

feelings and needs.

Acknowledging the need for healing is a crucial step towards breaking free from a toxic relationship. It requires self-reflection, honesty, and the willingness to prioritize your well-being. Here are some reasons why recognizing the need for healing is essential:

1. Protecting your mental and emotional health: Toxic relationships can have a severe impact on your mental and emotional well-being. Acknowledging the need for healing allows you to prioritize your mental health and take steps towards healing and recovery.

2. Breaking the cycle of toxicity: By recognizing the need for healing, you are taking a stand against toxic patterns and behaviors. It is an opportunity to break free from the cycle of toxicity and create a healthier future for yourself.

3. Rebuilding your self-esteem: Toxic relationships often erode your self-esteem and self-worth. Acknowledging the need for healing is the first step towards rebuilding your self-esteem and rediscovering your value.

4. Creating a healthier future: Recognizing the need for healing opens the door to a healthier and more fulfilling future. It allows you to let go of toxic relationships and make space for healthier connections and experiences.

5. Empowering yourself: Acknowledging the need for healing is an act of self-empowerment. It shows that you are taking control of your life and making choices that prioritize your well-being.

6. Learning from the experience: Recognizing the need for healing allows you to reflect on the toxic relationship and learn from the experience. It

provides an opportunity for personal growth and self-discovery.

7. Finding support and guidance: Once you acknowledge the need for healing, you can seek support and guidance from professionals, support groups, or trusted friends and family members. This support can be instrumental in your healing journey.

Remember, recognizing the need for healing is not a sign of weakness but a courageous step towards reclaiming your life and well-being. It may be challenging, but it is the first step towards breaking free from the toxic relationship and creating a healthier and happier future for yourself.

————

Seeking Professional Help

Seeking professional help is an essential step in healing from a toxic relationship. While it may be tempting to try to navigate the healing process on your own, the guidance and support of a trained professional can make a significant difference in your recovery journey. Therapists, counselors, and support groups can provide you with the tools and resources you need to heal, grow, and move forward.

Seeking professional help offers numerous benefits when recovering from a toxic relationship. Here are some of the key advantages:

One of the most significant benefits of seeking professional help is finding validation and understanding. A trained therapist or counselor can provide a safe and non-judgmental space for you to share your experiences and emotions. They can help you make sense of your feelings and validate your experiences, which can be incredibly empowering and healing.

Professionals have the knowledge and expertise to guide you

through the healing process. They can help you identify patterns, understand the dynamics of toxic relationships, and provide you with practical strategies to overcome the challenges you may face. Their guidance can help you gain clarity, develop healthier coping mechanisms, and make informed decisions about your future.

Recovering from a toxic relationship can be emotionally challenging. Having a professional who can provide emotional support and empathy can make a significant difference in your healing journey. They can help you process your emotions, navigate through grief and loss, and develop healthy ways to manage stress and anxiety.

A professional can equip you with a range of tools and coping strategies to help you heal and rebuild your life. They can teach you effective communication skills, boundary-setting techniques, and self-care practices. These tools will empower you to navigate future relationships more effectively and build a healthier and more fulfilling life.

Toxic relationships can often result in trauma, and seeking professional help ensures that you receive trauma-informed care. Trauma-informed therapists understand the impact of trauma on mental health and can provide specialized support to help you heal from the emotional wounds caused by the toxic relationship. They can guide you through the process of trauma recovery and help you regain a sense of safety and control.

When seeking professional help, it is crucial to choose the right therapist or counselor who specializes in trauma, relationships, or domestic abuse. Here are some factors to consider when selecting a professional:

Look for professionals who have experience working with individuals who have experienced toxic relationships or trauma. They should have a deep understanding of the dynamics of toxic relationships and the impact they can have on mental health. Consider seeking therapists who specialize in trauma, relationship counseling, or domestic abuse.

Building a strong therapeutic relationship is essential for your healing journey. It is crucial to find a therapist or counselor with whom you feel comfortable and can trust. Take the time to have an initial consultation or interview to assess their approach, values, and communication style. Trust your instincts and choose someone who feels like the right fit for you.

Ensure that the professional you choose is licensed and accredited. Check their credentials and verify their qualifications. This will give you confidence in their expertise and ensure that they adhere to professional standards and ethical guidelines.

Consider the practical aspects of seeking professional help, such as the location, availability, and cost. Choose a professional who is accessible and can accommodate your schedule. If in-person sessions are not feasible, explore the option of online therapy or counseling.

There are various types of professional help available to support you in healing from a toxic relationship. Here are some options to consider:

Individual therapy involves one-on-one sessions with a therapist or counselor. It provides a safe and confidential space for you to explore your experiences, emotions, and challenges. A therapist can help you gain insight into your patterns, develop coping strategies, and work through any trauma or emotional wounds.

Group therapy involves participating in therapy sessions with a small group of individuals who have experienced similar challenges. It provides a supportive and empathetic environment where you can share your experiences, learn from others, and gain a sense of community. Group therapy can be particularly beneficial for reducing feelings of isolation and building connections with others who have gone through similar experiences.

Support groups are facilitated by professionals or peers who have experienced toxic relationships. They offer a safe and non-judgmental space for individuals to share their stories, receive support, and learn from others. Support groups can provide a sense of validation, understanding, and camaraderie as you navigate your healing journey.

If you are in a toxic relationship and both partners are willing to work on the issues, couples therapy can be an option. A trained couples therapist can help you and your partner address the toxic dynamics, improve communication, and develop healthier relationship patterns. However, it is important to note that couples therapy is not recommended in cases of severe abuse or when there is a risk to your safety.

In some cases, seeking legal and financial support may be necessary, especially if you are dealing with issues such as divorce, child custody, or financial abuse. Consult with an attorney who specializes in family law to understand your rights and options. Additionally, financial advisors or counselors can provide guidance on managing your finances and rebuilding your financial independence.

Seeking professional help can be challenging, and there may be barriers that prevent you from reaching out. Here are some common barriers and strategies to overcome them:

The stigma surrounding therapy or counseling can make it difficult for some individuals to seek help. Remember that seeking professional help is a sign of strength and self-care, not weakness. Surround yourself with supportive individuals who understand the importance of seeking help and can provide encouragement.

Financial constraints can be a significant barrier to accessing professional help. However, many therapists offer sliding scale fees or reduced rates for individuals with limited financial resources. Research community mental health centers, non-profit organizations, or universities that may offer low-cost or free counseling services. Additionally, some insurance plans cover therapy or counseling, so check with your provider to understand your coverage.

If you have experienced a toxic relationship, it is natural to have trust issues and fear of opening up to others. Take your time to find a therapist or counselor who makes you feel safe and comfortable. Building trust may take time, but a skilled professional will understand and respect your boundaries.

Some individuals may not be aware of the resources available to them or may not recognize the need for professional help. Educate yourself about the benefits of therapy or counseling and the available options. Reach out to helplines, support groups, or trusted individuals who can provide information and guidance.

Remember, seeking professional help is an important step in your healing journey. It is a brave and empowering choice that can provide you with the support, guidance, and tools you need to heal, grow, and create a healthier and happier future.

Building a Support System

Building a support system is an essential step in healing from a toxic relationship. When you have been in a toxic relationship, it is common to feel isolated, alone, and unsure of who to turn to for help. However, surrounding yourself with a strong support system can provide you with the necessary emotional support, guidance, and encouragement to navigate the healing process. In this section, we will explore the importance of building a support system and provide practical tips on how to do so.

A support system consists of individuals who are there for you, offering emotional support, understanding, and encouragement. They can be friends, family members, therapists, support groups, or even online communities. Building a support system is crucial for several reasons:

1. Validation and Understanding: Having people who understand and validate your experiences can be incredibly empowering. They can provide a safe space for you to share your feelings and experiences without judgment.
2. Emotional Support: A support system can offer emotional support during difficult times. They can provide a listening ear, offer advice, and help you process your emotions.
3. Perspective and Guidance: Sometimes, when we are in the midst of a toxic relationship, it can be challenging to see things clearly. A support system can offer an outside perspective and provide guidance on navigating the healing process.
4. Accountability: Building a support system can help hold you accountable for your healing journey. They can remind you of your worth, encourage you to set boundaries, and support you in making positive changes.

When building a support system, it is essential to identify individuals who are supportive, understanding, and empathetic. Here are some qualities to look for in supportive individuals:
1. Empathy: Look for individuals who can empathize with your experiences and emotions. They should be

able to understand and validate your feelings without judgment.

2. Non-Judgmental Attitude: Supportive individuals should be non-judgmental and accepting of your choices and decisions. They should respect your autonomy and provide a safe space for you to express yourself.

3. Good Listeners: Seek out individuals who are good listeners. They should be able to give you their full attention, show genuine interest in your experiences, and provide thoughtful responses.

4. Trustworthy: It is crucial to build a support system with individuals you can trust. They should respect your privacy and maintain confidentiality.

5. Positive Influence: Surround yourself with individuals who have a positive outlook on life and can uplift and inspire you. Their positive energy can help you stay motivated and focused on your healing journey.

Building a support system takes time and effort. Here are some practical steps to help you build a strong support system:

1. Identify Potential Supportive Individuals: Make a list of people in your life who you believe could be supportive. This could include close friends, family members, therapists, or support groups.

2. Reach Out: Take the initiative to reach out to these individuals and express your need for support. Let them know that you value their presence in your life and that you would appreciate their support during your healing journey.

3. Join Support Groups: Consider joining support groups or online communities where you can connect with individuals who have gone through similar experiences. These groups can provide a sense of belonging and understanding.

4. Seek Professional Help: A therapist or counselor can be an invaluable part of your support system. They can provide professional guidance, help you process your emotions, and offer tools and strategies for healing.

5. Nurture Relationships: Invest time and effort into nurturing the relationships that are supportive and positive. Regularly communicate with your support system, share your progress, and seek their advice when needed.

6. Set Boundaries: It is essential to set boundaries within your support system. Communicate your needs and expectations clearly, and ensure that your boundaries are respected.

7. Diversify Your Support System: It can be helpful to have a diverse support system consisting of individuals with different perspectives and areas of expertise. This can provide you with a well-rounded support network.

Remember, building a support system is an ongoing process. It may take time to find the right individuals who truly understand and support you. Be patient with yourself and trust that with time, you will create a strong support system that will help you heal and thrive.

———

Self-Reflection and Personal Growth

Self-reflection and personal growth are essential components of healing from a toxic relationship. In order to move forward and create healthier relationships in the future, it is important to take the time to reflect on your experiences and understand how they have shaped you. This chapter will guide you through the process of self-reflection and provide strategies for personal growth.

Self-reflection involves looking back on your past experiences and examining the patterns and dynamics that were present in your toxic relationship. It is important to approach this process with compassion and without judgment. Here are some steps to help you reflect on your past:

1. Create a safe space: Find a quiet and comfortable space where you can reflect without distractions. This could be a cozy corner in your home or a peaceful outdoor setting.

2. Journaling: Start by journaling about your experiences in the toxic relationship. Write about the behaviors that were present, how they made you feel, and any patterns you noticed. This process can help you gain clarity and insight into the dynamics of the relationship.

3. Identify triggers: Reflect on the specific situations or behaviors that triggered negative emotions or reactions in you. Understanding your triggers can help you recognize patterns and develop strategies for managing them in the future.

4. Explore your emotions: Allow yourself to fully experience and process the emotions that arise as you reflect on your past. This may involve sadness, anger, or even relief. Give yourself permission to feel and express these emotions in a healthy way.

5. Recognize your role: Take responsibility for your own actions and behaviors within the toxic relationship. Reflect on how you may have contributed to the unhealthy dynamics and consider what changes you can make moving forward.

During the process of self-reflection, it is important to identify any patterns and beliefs that may have contributed to your involvement in a toxic relationship. These patterns and beliefs can stem from past experiences, childhood upbringing, or societal influences. Here are some steps to help you identify and challenge these patterns and beliefs:

1. Examine your past: Reflect on your childhood and past relationships to identify any recurring patterns or themes. Consider the dynamics that were present and how they may have influenced your beliefs about relationships.

2. Question your beliefs: Challenge any negative or limiting beliefs you may hold about yourself and relationships. Ask yourself if these beliefs are based on reality or if they are simply assumptions you have made.

3. Seek support: Reach out to a therapist or counselor who can help you explore and challenge your beliefs. They can provide guidance and support as you work through any negative patterns that may be holding you back.

4. Practice self-compassion: Be kind and gentle with yourself as you uncover and challenge these patterns and beliefs. Remember that personal growth is a journey, and it takes time and effort to make lasting changes.

Personal growth is a lifelong process that involves continuous learning, self-improvement, and self-discovery. It is an opportunity to develop new skills, expand your knowledge, and create a fulfilling life. Here are some strategies to help you cultivate personal growth after a toxic relationship:

1. Set goals: Identify areas of your life that you would like to improve or develop. Set specific, achievable goals that align with your values and aspirations. This could include pursuing a new hobby, learning a new skill, or focusing on your career.

2. Embrace learning: Be open to learning new things and expanding your knowledge. Take courses, read

books, or attend workshops that align with your interests and goals. This can help you gain new perspectives and insights.

3. Practice self-care: Prioritize self-care activities that nourish your mind, body, and soul. This could include engaging in regular exercise, practicing mindfulness or meditation, or engaging in activities that bring you joy and relaxation.

4. Seek support: Surround yourself with a supportive network of friends, family, or a support group who can provide encouragement and guidance as you navigate your personal growth journey. Share your goals and aspirations with them and seek their input and feedback.

5. Celebrate progress: Acknowledge and celebrate your progress along the way. Recognize the small steps you take towards personal growth and give yourself credit for the effort you put in. This will help you stay motivated and inspired to continue on your journey.

Remember, personal growth is a unique and individual process. It is important to honor your own pace and focus on what feels right for you. Embrace the opportunity to learn, grow, and create a life that is free from toxicity and filled with happiness and fulfillment.

CHAPTER 7: SETTING BOUNDARIES IN TOXIC RELATIONSHIPS

Understanding Boundaries

Boundaries play a crucial role in maintaining healthy relationships. They are the invisible lines that define where one person ends and another begins. In the context of toxic relationships, boundaries become even more important as they serve as a protective shield against harmful behaviors and actions. Understanding boundaries is essential for recognizing and addressing toxic dynamics in relationships.

Boundaries are the limits we set for ourselves and others in terms of what is acceptable and what is not. They define our personal space, emotional well-being, and values. Boundaries can be physical, emotional, mental, or even spiritual. They help us establish a sense of self and protect our autonomy.

In toxic relationships, boundaries are often violated or disregarded. Toxic individuals may push and manipulate boundaries to gain control and power over their partners. Without clear boundaries, it becomes difficult to maintain a healthy sense of self and establish a balanced dynamic in the relationship.

Setting and enforcing boundaries in toxic relationships is crucial for several reasons:

1. Self-Protection: Boundaries act as a shield, protecting us from emotional, physical, and psychological harm. They help us maintain our well-being and prevent toxic behaviors from affecting us deeply.
2. Preserving Autonomy: Boundaries allow us to maintain our individuality and independence within the relationship. They ensure that our needs, desires, and values are respected and honored.
3. Establishing Mutual Respect: Boundaries create a framework for mutual respect and healthy communication. They set the tone for how we expect to be treated and how we treat others.
4. Identifying Red Flags: Clear boundaries help us recognize red flags and warning signs of toxic behavior. When our boundaries are repeatedly violated, it serves as a clear indication that the relationship may be unhealthy and harmful.

Establishing and enforcing boundaries in toxic relationships can be challenging, but it is essential for our well-being and personal growth. Here are some steps to help you navigate this process:

1. Self-Reflection: Take time to reflect on your values, needs, and limits. Understand what is important to you and what you are willing to tolerate in a relationship. This self-awareness will serve as a foundation for setting boundaries.
2. Identify Boundaries: Identify the areas where you feel

your boundaries have been violated or where you need to establish new boundaries. This could include emotional space, personal time, communication, or physical boundaries.

3. Communicate Clearly: Once you have identified your boundaries, communicate them clearly and assertively to your partner. Use "I" statements to express your needs and expectations. For example, "I need alone time in the evenings to recharge, so I would appreciate it if you respect that."

4. Be Consistent: Consistency is key when it comes to enforcing boundaries. Stick to your boundaries and do not compromise them for the sake of the relationship. This will send a clear message that your boundaries are non-negotiable.

5. Set Consequences: Establish consequences for boundary violations. Communicate these consequences to your partner, so they understand the impact of their actions. For example, if your partner repeatedly crosses a certain boundary, you may need to consider taking a break or seeking professional help.

6. Seek Support: Reach out to trusted friends, family, or a therapist for support and guidance. They can provide an outside perspective and help you stay accountable to your boundaries.

When setting boundaries in a toxic relationship, it is common to face resistance and pushback from the toxic individual. They may try to manipulate, guilt-trip, or invalidate your boundaries. Here are some strategies to navigate these challenges:

1. Stay Firm: Remain firm in your boundaries and do not let the toxic individual sway you. Remember that your well-being is a priority, and you have the right to set boundaries that protect you.

2. Practice Self-Care: Engage in self-care activities to

nurture yourself during this challenging time. This will help you stay grounded and maintain your emotional well-being.

3. Seek Professional Help: If the resistance and pushback become overwhelming, consider seeking professional help from a therapist or counselor. They can provide guidance and support as you navigate the complexities of a toxic relationship.

4. Evaluate the Relationship: Continuously evaluate the relationship and assess whether the toxic dynamics are improving or worsening. If the toxic behaviors persist despite your efforts to set boundaries, it may be necessary to consider ending the relationship for your own well-being.

Remember, setting and enforcing boundaries is an ongoing process. It requires self-awareness, assertiveness, and a commitment to your own well-being. By establishing healthy boundaries, you can create a safer and more fulfilling life for yourself, free from the toxicity of unhealthy relationships.

———

Why Boundaries are Important in Toxic Relationships

Setting boundaries is crucial in any relationship, but it becomes even more essential in toxic relationships. When you are in a toxic relationship, your emotional and mental well-being is at stake. Boundaries act as a protective shield, helping you establish and maintain a sense of self and protect yourself from further harm. In this section, we will explore why boundaries are important in toxic relationships and how they can empower you to create a healthier dynamic.

Toxic relationships often involve emotional manipulation, control, and abuse. Without clear boundaries, you may find yourself constantly subjected to emotional turmoil and manipulation. By setting boundaries, you establish limits on what behavior is acceptable and what is not. This empowers you to protect your emotional well-being and maintain a sense of control over your own emotions.

Boundaries help you define what you will and will not tolerate in a relationship. They allow you to communicate your needs, desires, and limits to your partner. By clearly expressing your boundaries, you create a framework for a healthier and more respectful relationship.

In toxic relationships, one partner often exerts control over the other, leaving the victim feeling powerless and dependent. Boundaries help you regain your autonomy and assert your individuality. They allow you to establish a sense of self separate from the toxic dynamics of the relationship.

By setting boundaries, you reclaim your power and assert your right to make decisions for yourself. This can be a transformative process, as it helps you break free from the cycle of control and manipulation. Boundaries enable you to prioritize your own needs and desires, rather than constantly sacrificing them for the sake of the toxic relationship.

Toxic relationships are characterized by poor communication patterns, such as constant criticism, blame-shifting, and defensiveness. Boundaries provide a framework for healthy communication by setting expectations for respectful and open dialogue.

When you establish boundaries around communication, you create a safe space for expressing your thoughts and feelings without fear of judgment or retaliation. Boundaries also help you establish consequences for disrespectful or abusive communication, which can encourage your partner to reflect on their behavior and make positive changes.

In some cases, toxic relationships can escalate to physical or sexual abuse. Boundaries play a crucial role in protecting your physical safety. By clearly defining what is acceptable and what is not, you establish a line that should never be crossed.

Setting physical boundaries communicates that any form of physical or sexual violence is unacceptable. It empowers you to prioritize your safety and well-being above all else. If your boundaries are violated, it is important to seek help and remove yourself from the dangerous situation as soon as possible.

Toxic relationships can have a severe impact on your mental health, leading to anxiety, depression, and low self-esteem. Boundaries act as a protective barrier, helping you preserve your mental well-being.
By setting boundaries, you create a space where you can prioritize self-care and engage in activities that promote your mental health. Boundaries also allow you to limit exposure to toxic behaviors and negative influences, reducing the emotional toll they have on you.
Boundaries are not only about protecting yourself; they also provide an opportunity for personal growth. By setting and enforcing boundaries, you develop a stronger sense of self and gain confidence in your ability to advocate for your needs.

As you establish and maintain boundaries, you learn to trust your instincts and prioritize your own well-being. This process of self-discovery and personal growth can be transformative, leading to increased self-esteem and a greater sense of empowerment.

Boundaries are essential in toxic relationships as they protect your emotional well-being, help you regain autonomy, establish healthy communication, protect your physical safety, preserve your mental health, and empower personal growth. Setting and enforcing boundaries is a powerful tool for creating a healthier dynamic and breaking free from the toxic patterns that have held you back. Remember, you deserve to be in a relationship that is built on respect, trust, and mutual support.

———

How to Establish and Enforce Boundaries

Establishing and enforcing boundaries is crucial when dealing with toxic relationships. Boundaries are the limits and guidelines we set for ourselves to protect our emotional, mental, and physical well-being. They help us define what is acceptable and what is not in our relationships. In a toxic relationship, boundaries are often disregarded or violated, leading to feelings of resentment, frustration, and even harm. Learning how to establish and enforce boundaries is essential for creating healthier and more fulfilling relationships. Here are some steps to help you establish and enforce boundaries in a toxic relationship:

Before setting boundaries, it is important to reflect on your needs and values. Take some time to identify what is important to you in a relationship and what behaviors or actions are unacceptable. Consider your emotional, mental, and physical well-being and think about the things that make you feel uncomfortable or violated. Reflecting on your needs and values will help you establish boundaries that align with your personal values and promote your overall well-being.

Once you have identified your boundaries, it is crucial to communicate them clearly to the other person. Choose a time when both of you are calm and can have an open and honest conversation. Use "I" statements to express how certain behaviors or actions make you feel and explain why those behaviors are not acceptable to you. Be assertive but respectful in your communication, making sure to express your boundaries in a clear and concise manner.

Establishing boundaries is not enough; you also need to be firm and consistent in enforcing them. It is common for toxic individuals to test boundaries and push limits. They may try to manipulate or guilt-trip you into disregarding your boundaries. It is important to stay firm and not give in to their tactics. Consistently reinforce your boundaries by reminding the other person of your expectations and the consequences of crossing those boundaries. By being firm and consistent, you send a clear message that your boundaries are non-negotiable.

Setting consequences for boundary violations is an important part of enforcing boundaries. Consequences help reinforce the importance of respecting your boundaries and discourage the other person from crossing them. Clearly communicate the consequences to the other person and make sure they understand the potential outcomes of disregarding your boundaries. Consequences can vary depending on the situation and the severity of the boundary violation. They can range from taking a break from the relationship to seeking professional help or even ending the relationship altogether. Choose consequences that align with your values and prioritize your well-being.

Establishing and enforcing boundaries can be challenging, especially in toxic relationships where the other person may resist or push back against your boundaries. Seeking support from trusted friends, family members, or a therapist can be incredibly helpful. They can provide you with guidance, validation, and encouragement as you navigate the process of setting and enforcing boundaries. They can also offer an outside perspective and help you stay accountable to your boundaries.

Taking care of yourself is essential when establishing and enforcing boundaries in a toxic relationship. Prioritize self-care activities that promote your well-being and help you maintain your emotional and mental health. Engage in activities that bring you joy, practice relaxation techniques, and make time for self-reflection and self-care. By prioritizing your own well-being, you are better equipped to establish and enforce boundaries in your relationships.

When setting boundaries in a toxic relationship, it is important to be prepared for resistance and pushback from the other person. Toxic individuals may not respond positively to your boundaries and may try to manipulate or guilt-trip you into disregarding them. It is crucial to stay strong and not let their tactics sway you. Remember that you have the right to set boundaries and prioritize your well-being. Stay firm, seek support from others, and remind yourself of your worth and the importance of your boundaries.

Boundaries are not set in stone and may need to be reevaluated and adjusted as the relationship progresses. As you gain more clarity and insight into your needs and values, you may find that certain boundaries need to be modified or expanded. It is important to regularly assess your boundaries and make adjustments as necessary. Remember that boundaries are a dynamic process and should evolve as you grow and change.

Establishing and enforcing boundaries in a toxic relationship can be challenging, but it is essential for your well-being and personal growth. By reflecting on your needs and values, clearly communicating your boundaries, being firm and consistent, setting consequences, seeking support, practicing self-care, and being prepared for resistance, you can create healthier and more fulfilling relationships. Remember that you deserve to be in relationships that respect and honor your boundaries.

———

Dealing with Resistance

and Pushback

Dealing with resistance and pushback can be one of the most challenging aspects of setting boundaries in a toxic relationship. When you start establishing and enforcing boundaries, it is common to encounter resistance from the other person. This resistance can manifest in various ways, such as denial, anger, manipulation, or even threats. It is important to be prepared for these reactions and have strategies in place to navigate them effectively.

Resistance is a natural response when someone feels their control or power is being challenged. In a toxic relationship, the toxic person may have become accustomed to having their needs and desires prioritized over yours. When you begin to set boundaries, it disrupts this dynamic and threatens their sense of control. As a result, they may resist your attempts to establish healthier boundaries.

It is crucial to understand that resistance is not a reflection of your worth or the validity of your boundaries. It is a defense mechanism employed by the toxic person to maintain the status quo. Recognizing this can help you approach the situation with empathy and clarity.

When faced with resistance and pushback, it is essential to stay firm and consistent in upholding your boundaries. The toxic person may try to test your resolve by pushing the boundaries or attempting to manipulate you into relenting. It is crucial not to give in to their tactics.

Remind yourself of the reasons why you established these boundaries in the first place. Remember that you deserve to be treated with respect and that setting boundaries is an act of self-care. Stay committed to your boundaries and do not waver, even if the toxic person becomes angry or tries to guilt-trip you.

When dealing with resistance, it is important to communicate your boundaries clearly and calmly. Avoid getting defensive or engaging in arguments. Instead, express your boundaries assertively and without aggression. Use "I" statements to convey your needs and expectations.

For example, instead of saying, "You always make me feel guilty," say, "I feel guilty when you say hurtful things about me." By using "I" statements, you take ownership of your feelings and avoid blaming the other person. This approach can help defuse potential conflicts and keep the conversation focused on your boundaries.

In some cases, setting consequences for crossing your boundaries can be an effective way to deal with resistance. Consequences provide a clear understanding of the potential outcomes if the toxic person continues to disregard your boundaries. It is important to establish consequences that are reasonable and enforceable.

For example, if the toxic person repeatedly violates your privacy by going through your personal belongings, a consequence could be limiting their access to your personal space. Communicate the consequences clearly and follow through with them if necessary. Consistency in enforcing consequences will help reinforce the importance of respecting your boundaries.

Dealing with resistance and pushback can be emotionally draining and challenging. It is crucial to seek support from trusted friends, family, or a therapist who can provide guidance and validation. Share your experiences and feelings with them, and seek their advice on how to navigate the resistance effectively.

Having a support system can provide you with the strength and encouragement you need to stay firm in upholding your boundaries. They can also offer an outside perspective and help you recognize any manipulative tactics or gaslighting that may be used against you.

Dealing with resistance and pushback can be emotionally taxing, so it is important to prioritize self-care during this time. Engage in activities that bring you joy and help you relax. Take care of your physical and emotional well-being by getting enough sleep, eating nutritious meals, and engaging in regular exercise.

Additionally, practicing self-compassion is crucial. Remind yourself that setting boundaries is an act of self-love and that you deserve to be treated with respect. Be patient with yourself and acknowledge that navigating resistance is a challenging process. Celebrate your progress and give yourself credit for the strength and courage it takes to stand up for yourself.

If the resistance and pushback become overwhelming or escalate to a dangerous level, it may be necessary to seek professional help. A therapist or counselor can provide you with the necessary tools and support to navigate the challenges of setting boundaries in a toxic relationship. They can help you develop strategies to manage resistance effectively and ensure your safety.

Remember, seeking professional help is not a sign of weakness but a proactive step towards healing and growth. A trained professional can offer guidance tailored to your specific situation and help you develop a plan to navigate the resistance and pushback you may encounter.

Dealing with resistance and pushback in a toxic relationship can be incredibly challenging, but it is essential for your well-being and personal growth. Stay firm in upholding your boundaries, seek support, and prioritize self-care. Remember that you deserve to be treated with respect and that setting boundaries is an act of self-love and self-preservation.

CHAPTER 8: ENDING A TOXIC RELATIONSHIP

*Recognizing When It's Time
to End the Relationship*

Recognizing a toxic relationship can be challenging, especially when you are emotionally invested in the person or situation. However, it is crucial to be able to identify the signs and patterns of toxicity in order to protect your well-being and make informed decisions about your relationship. Here are some key indicators that can help you recognize when it's time to end a toxic relationship:

1. Lack of respect and boundaries: In a healthy relationship, there is mutual respect and an understanding of personal boundaries. In a toxic relationship, one or both partners may consistently disregard each other's boundaries, leading to feelings of disrespect and violation.
2. Constant criticism and belittling: Toxic relationships often involve a pattern of criticism, belittling, and demeaning behavior. If your partner consistently puts you down, insults you, or undermines your self-esteem, it is a clear sign of toxicity.

3. Manipulation and control: Toxic relationships are characterized by manipulation and control. If your partner constantly manipulates your emotions, gaslights you, or tries to control your actions, thoughts, or decisions, it is a red flag that the relationship is unhealthy.

4. Emotional and verbal abuse: Emotional and verbal abuse can be just as damaging as physical abuse. If your partner regularly engages in name-calling, yelling, threatening, or using manipulative tactics to control your emotions, it is a clear indication of a toxic relationship.

5. Lack of trust and honesty: Trust and honesty are the foundation of a healthy relationship. In a toxic relationship, there is often a lack of trust, with one or both partners consistently lying, hiding information, or betraying each other's trust.

6. Constant negativity and draining energy: Toxic relationships tend to be filled with negativity, constant arguments, and a draining of emotional energy. If you find yourself feeling exhausted, anxious, or constantly on edge when you are with your partner, it may be a sign that the relationship is toxic.

7. Isolation from friends and family: Toxic partners often try to isolate their significant other from their support system. If you notice that your partner discourages you from spending time with friends and family, or if they try to control who you can and cannot see, it is a warning sign of a toxic relationship.

8. Lack of reciprocity and imbalance: Healthy relationships are built on mutual give and take, with both partners contributing equally to the relationship. In a toxic relationship, there is often an imbalance, with one partner consistently taking more than they give and showing little regard for the

other person's needs and desires.

9. Feeling trapped and unable to be yourself: In a toxic relationship, you may feel like you have to constantly walk on eggshells or hide your true self in order to avoid conflict or criticism. If you feel like you cannot be your authentic self or express your true thoughts and feelings without fear of judgment or backlash, it is a sign that the relationship is toxic.

10. Persistent unhappiness and dissatisfaction: Ultimately, if you find yourself consistently unhappy, unfulfilled, or dissatisfied in your relationship, it may be a strong indication that it is toxic. A healthy relationship should bring joy, support, and fulfillment to your life, not constant negativity and unhappiness.

It is important to remember that recognizing the signs of a toxic relationship is the first step towards healing and creating a healthier future for yourself. If you identify with any of these signs, it may be time to consider ending the relationship and seeking support to help you navigate the process.

Planning for Safety

When you have come to the realization that you are in a toxic relationship and have made the decision to end it, it is crucial to prioritize your safety. Ending a toxic relationship can be a challenging and potentially dangerous process, so it is important to have a plan in place to ensure your well-being. Planning for safety involves taking proactive steps to protect yourself physically, emotionally, and financially. Here are some important considerations and strategies to help you plan for safety when ending a toxic relationship:

Before taking any action, it is essential to assess the level of risk involved in ending the toxic relationship. Every situation is unique, and the level of danger can vary depending on factors such as the history of violence or abuse, the presence of weapons, and the aggressor's behavior patterns. If you feel that your safety is at immediate risk, it is crucial to reach out to local authorities or a domestic violence hotline for immediate assistance.

One of the first steps in planning for safety is to secure a safe space where you can go to seek refuge from the toxic relationship. This may involve finding a trusted friend or family member who can provide temporary shelter, or it may require seeking assistance from a local shelter or safe house. It is important to have a place where you can feel secure and protected as you navigate the process of ending the toxic relationship.

Building a strong support network is vital when planning for safety. Reach out to friends, family, or support groups who can provide emotional support, guidance, and assistance during this challenging time. Let them know about your situation and your plans to end the toxic relationship, so they can be prepared to help you when needed. Having a support network in place can provide you with the strength and encouragement you need to move forward.

Keeping a record of any incidents of abuse or toxic behavior can be crucial when planning for safety. Documenting dates, times, and details of incidents can serve as evidence if legal action becomes necessary. It is important to include any physical injuries, photographs, or medical reports related to the abuse. This documentation can help support your case and protect your rights during the process of ending the toxic relationship.

In cases where there is a significant risk to your safety, obtaining a restraining order or protective order can provide legal protection. Consult with a lawyer or seek assistance from a local domestic violence organization to understand the legal options available to you. They can guide you through the process of obtaining a restraining order and provide information on how to enforce it if necessary.

Financial independence is crucial when planning for safety. If you are financially dependent on the toxic partner, it is important to take steps to become financially self-sufficient. This may involve finding employment, seeking educational opportunities, or accessing resources such as job training programs or financial assistance. Having financial independence will not only provide you with the means to support yourself but also give you the freedom to make decisions without being controlled or manipulated by the toxic partner.

If you have children involved in the toxic relationship, their safety should be a top priority. Develop a safety plan specifically tailored to their needs. This may involve discussing the situation with their school or daycare providers, informing trusted family members or friends about the situation, and teaching your children about safety measures such as knowing emergency phone numbers and identifying safe places to go in case of danger. It is important to shield children from witnessing or experiencing any further harm.

When planning for safety, it is crucial to consider communication and social media safety. Change passwords to your email, social media accounts, and any other online platforms to prevent the toxic partner from accessing your personal information. Be cautious about sharing your plans or whereabouts on social media, as this information can be used against you. Consider blocking or limiting contact with the toxic partner on all communication channels to minimize the risk of harassment or further abuse.

In situations where there is an immediate threat to your safety, it is important to have an emergency exit strategy in place. This may involve identifying escape routes in your home, keeping a bag packed with essential items such as identification documents, money, and clothing, and having a plan for where to go in case of an emergency. Share this plan with trusted individuals who can provide assistance if needed.

When planning for safety, it is essential to seek professional help from therapists, counselors, or support groups specializing in domestic violence or toxic relationships. These professionals can provide guidance, support, and resources to help you navigate the process of ending the toxic relationship safely. They can also assist you in developing a personalized safety plan based on your specific circumstances.

Remember, planning for safety is a critical step in ending a toxic relationship. It is important to take these precautions seriously and seek assistance from professionals and support networks. Your safety and well-being should always be the top priority as you work towards breaking free from the toxicity and creating a healthier and happier life for yourself.

———

Breaking Free from the Toxic Relationship

Breaking free from a toxic relationship can be a challenging and emotional process. It requires courage, self-reflection, and a commitment to your own well-being. In this section, we will explore some practical steps you can take to break free from a toxic relationship and begin your journey towards healing and freedom.

The first step in breaking free from a toxic relationship is to acknowledge and accept that the relationship is toxic. This can be a difficult realization, as it may involve confronting painful truths about the dynamics of the relationship and the impact it has had on your well-being. However, it is essential to recognize the toxicity in order to take the necessary steps towards healing.

Take some time to reflect on the patterns of behavior in the relationship and how they have affected you. Consider the signs of toxicity that you have learned about in earlier chapters, such as manipulation, control, abuse, and gaslighting. Be honest with yourself about the negative impact the relationship has had on your mental, emotional, and physical health.

Breaking free from a toxic relationship can be an overwhelming and isolating experience. It is important to reach out for support during this time. Surround yourself with trusted friends, family members, or support groups who can provide a safe and non-judgmental space for you to share your experiences and emotions.

Consider seeking professional help from a therapist or counselor who specializes in trauma and relationship issues. They can provide guidance, validation, and tools to help you navigate the process of breaking free from the toxic relationship. Therapy can also help you address any underlying issues, such as codependency or low self-esteem, that may have contributed to your involvement in the toxic relationship.

Breaking free from a toxic relationship can sometimes be dangerous, especially if there is a history of physical or emotional abuse. It is crucial to prioritize your safety during this process. If you feel that you are in immediate danger, reach out to local authorities or a domestic violence hotline for assistance.

Create a safety plan that includes practical steps to protect yourself. This may involve changing locks, securing important documents, and informing trusted individuals about your situation. Consider developing a code word or signal with a trusted friend or family member that indicates you are in danger and need help.

Setting and enforcing boundaries is a crucial part of breaking free from a toxic relationship. Clearly communicate your boundaries to the toxic person and be firm in upholding them. This may involve limiting or cutting off contact with the toxic person, blocking them on social media, or changing your phone number.

It is important to remember that setting boundaries is not about punishing the other person, but rather about protecting yourself and creating a healthy space for healing. Be prepared for resistance and pushback from the toxic person, as they may try to manipulate or guilt-trip you into maintaining the toxic relationship. Stay strong and remind yourself of your worth and the importance of your well-being.

Breaking free from a toxic relationship can be emotionally draining, so it is crucial to prioritize self-care during this time. Take care of your physical and emotional well-being by engaging in activities that bring you joy and relaxation. This may include exercise, meditation, spending time in nature, or pursuing hobbies and interests.

Practice self-compassion and be gentle with yourself as you navigate the healing process. Surround yourself with positive influences and engage in activities that promote self-growth and personal development. Consider journaling or therapy to process your emotions and gain clarity on your experiences.

Breaking free from a toxic relationship is not a one-time event, but rather a journey towards healing and self-discovery. It is important to stay committed to your healing process and be patient with yourself. Understand that healing takes time and that there may be setbacks along the way.

Continue to seek support from trusted individuals and professionals who can guide you through the healing process. Engage in self-reflection and personal growth to gain a deeper understanding of yourself and your needs in relationships. Celebrate your progress and acknowledge the strength and resilience it takes to break free from a toxic relationship.

Remember, you deserve to be in a healthy and loving relationship. By breaking free from a toxic relationship, you are taking a courageous step towards reclaiming your happiness and well-being.

––––

Recovering and Moving Forward

Recovering from a toxic relationship can be a challenging and emotional journey. It is important to remember that healing takes time and patience. Moving forward after leaving a toxic relationship requires self-reflection, self-care, and a commitment to personal growth. In this section, we will explore some strategies and techniques to help you recover and thrive after ending a toxic relationship.

One of the first steps in recovering from a toxic relationship is to acknowledge and embrace your emotions. It is normal to experience a wide range of emotions such as anger, sadness, confusion, and even relief. Allow yourself to feel these emotions without judgment or guilt. Give yourself permission to grieve the loss of the relationship and the dreams you had for it. Remember that healing is a process, and it is okay to take the time you need to heal.

Building a support system is crucial during the recovery process. Reach out to trusted friends, family members, or support groups who can provide a safe space for you to share your experiences and emotions. Surround yourself with people who will listen without judgment and offer support and encouragement. Consider seeking professional help from a therapist or counselor who specializes in trauma and relationship issues. They can provide guidance and tools to help you navigate the healing process.

Self-care is essential for healing and moving forward after a toxic relationship. Take time to prioritize your physical, emotional, and mental well-being. Engage in activities that bring you joy and relaxation, such as exercise, meditation, journaling, or spending time in nature. Nourish your body with healthy food and make sure to get enough restful sleep. Set boundaries with yourself and others to ensure that you are taking care of your needs and not overextending yourself.

It is common for survivors of toxic relationships to experience feelings of guilt and shame. You may question your own judgment or blame yourself for staying in the relationship for as long as you did. It is important to remember that you are not to blame for the toxic dynamics in the relationship. Recognize that you did the best you could with the knowledge and resources you had at the time. Practice self-compassion and remind yourself that you deserve love, respect, and happiness.

After leaving a toxic relationship, it is crucial to establish and enforce healthy boundaries. Take the time to reflect on what you need and want in your relationships moving forward. Communicate your boundaries clearly and assertively to others. Be prepared for resistance or pushback from those who may have benefited from your lack of boundaries in the past. Remember that setting boundaries is an act of self-care and self-respect.

Leaving a toxic relationship provides an opportunity for self-discovery and personal growth. Take the time to reconnect with yourself and explore your interests, passions, and values. Engage in activities that bring you joy and allow you to express your authentic self. Rediscover your strengths and celebrate your accomplishments. Use this time to focus on your personal growth and create a life that aligns with your values and aspirations.

Forgiveness is a powerful tool in the healing process. It is important to forgive yourself for any perceived mistakes or shortcomings in the relationship. Remember that you were doing the best you could with the knowledge and resources you had at the time. Forgiving the other person involved in the toxic relationship is also important for your own healing. This does not mean condoning their behavior, but rather releasing the anger and resentment that may be holding you back from moving forward.

If you find that the healing process is overwhelming or if you are struggling to move forward, consider seeking professional help. A therapist or counselor can provide guidance, support, and tools to help you navigate the challenges of recovering from a toxic relationship. They can help you process your emotions, develop healthy coping strategies, and work through any unresolved trauma. Remember that seeking help is a sign of strength, and it can greatly accelerate your healing journey.

Practicing gratitude and focusing on the positive aspects of your life can help shift your mindset and promote healing. Take time each day to reflect on the things you are grateful for, no matter how small. Surround yourself with positive influences, whether it be through uplifting books, podcasts, or supportive friends. Cultivating a positive mindset can help you regain your sense of self-worth and attract healthier relationships in the future.

Moving forward after a toxic relationship requires courage and resilience. Celebrate your progress and acknowledge the strength it took to leave the toxic relationship. Trust yourself and your instincts as you navigate new relationships and opportunities. Remember that you deserve love, respect, and happiness. Embrace the lessons you have learned and use them as stepping stones to create a life filled with joy, fulfillment, and healthy relationships.

Recovering from a toxic relationship is a journey that takes time, patience, and self-compassion. By embracing your emotions, seeking support, practicing self-care, setting boundaries, and focusing on personal growth, you can heal and move forward with confidence. Remember that you are not alone, and there is hope for a brighter future.

CHAPTER 9: NAVIGATING CO-PARENTING IN A TOXIC RELATIONSHIP

*The Challenges of Co-Parenting
in a Toxic Relationship*

Co-parenting can be challenging even in the best of circumstances, but when you are co-parenting with a toxic ex-partner, the challenges can feel overwhelming. In a toxic relationship, the dynamics between the parents are unhealthy and often characterized by manipulation, control, and conflict. These toxic behaviors can have a detrimental impact on the well-being of both the parents and the children involved.

One of the most significant challenges of co-parenting in a toxic relationship is the negative impact it can have on the children. Children who are exposed to toxic co-parenting often experience emotional distress, confusion, and a sense of instability. They may witness frequent arguments, hostility, and even violence between their parents, which can lead to feelings of fear, anxiety, and low self-esteem.

Children in toxic co-parenting situations may also be caught in the middle of their parents' conflicts, being used as pawns or messengers. This can place an immense burden on them, as they may feel torn between their parents and forced to choose sides. The constant exposure to conflict and tension can disrupt their sense of security and hinder their emotional and psychological development.

Effective communication is crucial in co-parenting, but in a toxic relationship, communication can be extremely challenging. Toxic ex-partners may engage in manipulative tactics, such as gaslighting, where they distort the truth or deny their actions to confuse and control the other parent. They may also use verbal abuse, insults, or threats to intimidate and undermine the other parent's authority.

In a toxic co-parenting relationship, it can be difficult to have civil and productive conversations about parenting decisions, schedules, or other important matters. The toxic dynamics often lead to power struggles and an inability to reach agreements, which can create a hostile and unstable environment for both the parents and the children.

Coordinating parenting styles can be a challenge even in healthy co-parenting relationships, but in a toxic relationship, it can be even more complicated. Toxic ex-partners may have different values, beliefs, and approaches to parenting, which can lead to conflicts and disagreements about how to raise the children.

In a toxic co-parenting relationship, one parent may try to undermine the other parent's authority or manipulate the children against the other parent. This can create confusion and inconsistency in parenting, making it difficult for the children to establish a sense of stability and routine.

Co-parenting in a toxic relationship can take a toll on the emotional and mental health of both parents. The constant exposure to toxic behaviors, conflicts, and power struggles can lead to high levels of stress, anxiety, and depression. It can be emotionally draining to navigate the challenges of co-parenting with someone who is manipulative, controlling, or abusive.

The toxic dynamics of the relationship can also trigger feelings of guilt, shame, and self-doubt in the targeted parent. They may question their parenting abilities and constantly second-guess themselves due to the constant criticism and invalidation from their toxic ex-partner.

Co-parenting in a toxic relationship can also present legal and financial challenges. Toxic ex-partners may use the legal system as a tool for control or revenge, making false accusations or dragging out legal proceedings to exert power over the other parent. This can result in lengthy and costly court battles, which can further exacerbate the stress and strain on both parents.

Financial challenges may also arise in toxic co-parenting relationships. One parent may refuse to contribute financially or use money as a means of control. This can create financial instability for the parent who is primarily responsible for the children's day-to-day needs.

Despite the challenges, it is possible to navigate co-parenting in a toxic relationship in a way that minimizes the negative impact on both the parents and the children. Here are some strategies to consider:

1. Focus on the children: Keep the best interests of the children at the forefront of your decision-making. Put aside personal differences and prioritize their well-being.
2. Establish clear boundaries: Set clear boundaries with your toxic ex-partner to protect yourself and your

children from their toxic behaviors. Clearly define expectations and consequences for crossing those boundaries.

3. Communicate through a neutral platform: If direct communication with your toxic ex-partner is too challenging, consider using a neutral platform, such as a co-parenting app or email, to communicate about parenting matters.

4. Seek support: Reach out to friends, family, or a support group who can provide emotional support and guidance during this challenging time. Consider seeking therapy or counseling to help you navigate the emotional impact of the toxic relationship.

5. Document everything: Keep a record of all communication, incidents, and interactions with your toxic ex-partner. This documentation can be useful in legal proceedings or custody disputes.

6. Focus on self-care: Take care of yourself physically, emotionally, and mentally. Engage in activities that bring you joy and help you recharge. Prioritize self-care to ensure you have the energy and resilience to navigate the challenges of co-parenting.

Remember, co-parenting in a toxic relationship is not easy, but by prioritizing the well-being of your children and taking steps to protect yourself, you can create a healthier environment for both you and your children.

―――

Protecting Children from Toxicity

When co-parenting in a toxic relationship, it is crucial to prioritize the well-being and safety of your children. Children who are exposed to toxic relationships can experience significant emotional and psychological harm, which can have long-lasting effects on their development and overall happiness.

As a parent, it is your responsibility to protect your children from the toxicity of the relationship and create a healthy environment for them to thrive in.

Children are highly perceptive and can sense tension and conflict within the household. Even if they are not directly involved in the toxic dynamics, they can still be deeply affected by them. It is important to recognize the signs of how a toxic relationship can impact children:

1. Emotional distress: Children may exhibit signs of anxiety, depression, or withdrawal. They may become more irritable, have difficulty sleeping, or experience changes in appetite.
2. Behavioral changes: Children may display aggressive or defiant behavior, have difficulty concentrating, or experience a decline in academic performance. They may also exhibit regressive behaviors such as bedwetting or thumb-sucking.
3. Low self-esteem: Children who witness toxic relationships may develop a negative self-image and struggle with self-confidence. They may blame themselves for the problems in the relationship or feel unworthy of love and affection.
4. Difficulty forming healthy relationships: Growing up in a toxic environment can impact a child's ability to form healthy relationships in the future. They may struggle with trust, have difficulty expressing emotions, or engage in unhealthy relationship patterns themselves.

As a parent, it is essential to create a safe and healthy environment for your children, free from the toxicity of the relationship. Here are some strategies to protect your children from the negative effects of a toxic relationship:

1. Shield them from conflict: Minimize your children's exposure to arguments and conflicts between you and your co-parent. Avoid discussing sensitive topics or engaging in heated debates in front of them. Create a peaceful and harmonious atmosphere whenever possible.
2. Provide stability and routine: Establishing a consistent routine can provide a sense of stability and security for your children. Maintain regular mealtimes, bedtimes, and activities to create a predictable and structured environment.
3. Encourage open communication: Create a safe space for your children to express their feelings and concerns. Encourage them to talk about their emotions and validate their experiences. Let them know that it is okay to feel upset or confused and reassure them that they are not responsible for the problems in the relationship.
4. Model healthy behavior: Be a positive role model for your children by demonstrating healthy communication, conflict resolution, and emotional regulation. Show them what a healthy relationship looks like by treating others with respect, empathy, and kindness.
5. Foster a support network: Surround yourself and your children with a supportive network of friends, family, and professionals who can provide emotional support and guidance. Seek out therapy or counseling for yourself and your children to help navigate the challenges of co-parenting in a toxic relationship.

Co-parenting in a toxic relationship can be challenging, but it is possible to create a healthy environment for your children by implementing effective co-parenting strategies:

1. Establish clear boundaries: Clearly define boundaries with your co-parent to ensure that your children's well-being is prioritized. Agree on rules and expectations regarding discipline, communication, and decision-making. Stick to these boundaries and hold each other accountable.

2. Communicate through neutral channels: If direct communication with your co-parent is difficult, consider using neutral channels such as email or a co-parenting app to communicate about important matters regarding your children. Keep the focus on the children and avoid engaging in personal attacks or arguments.

3. Create a parenting plan: Develop a comprehensive parenting plan that outlines the responsibilities and schedules for both parents. This plan should address custody arrangements, visitation schedules, and decision-making processes. Having a clear plan in place can minimize conflicts and provide structure for your children.

4. Maintain consistency: Consistency is key in co-parenting. Try to maintain similar rules, routines, and expectations in both households to provide stability for your children. This consistency can help them feel secure and reduce confusion or anxiety.

In some cases, co-parenting in a toxic relationship may require legal intervention or mediation to ensure the safety and well-being of your children. If you believe that your children are at risk or that the toxic dynamics are negatively impacting their lives, it is important to seek legal support. Consult with a family law attorney who specializes in child custody and co-parenting issues to explore your options.

Mediation can also be a valuable tool in resolving conflicts and establishing effective co-parenting strategies. A trained mediator can help facilitate communication and guide both parents towards finding mutually beneficial solutions. Mediation can provide a neutral and safe space for discussions, allowing for the best interests of the children to be prioritized.

Remember, protecting your children from the toxicity of a relationship is essential for their well-being and development. By creating a safe and healthy environment, implementing effective co-parenting strategies, and seeking the necessary support, you can help your children thrive despite the challenges of co-parenting in a toxic relationship.

Co-Parenting Strategies for a Healthy Environment

Co-parenting in a toxic relationship can be incredibly challenging and emotionally draining. However, it is essential to prioritize the well-being of your children and create a healthy environment for them to thrive. While it may seem difficult, there are strategies you can implement to navigate co-parenting in a toxic relationship effectively.

When co-parenting in a toxic relationship, it is crucial to prioritize the needs of your children above all else. Remember that they are innocent bystanders in the toxic dynamics between you and your ex-partner. By focusing on their well-being, you can create a safe and nurturing environment for them.

Ensure that your decisions and actions are guided by what is best for your children. This means setting aside your personal feelings and conflicts with your ex-partner and making choices that promote their emotional, physical, and psychological well-being.

Children thrive on stability and routine, especially in the midst of a toxic relationship. Establishing consistent schedules and routines can provide a sense of security and predictability for your children. This can help them feel more grounded and stable, even in the face of the toxic dynamics between their parents.

Work with your ex-partner to create a co-parenting schedule that allows for regular and consistent contact with both parents. Stick to the agreed-upon schedule as much as possible to minimize disruptions and provide a sense of stability for your children.

Effective communication is key to successful co-parenting in any situation, but it becomes even more critical in a toxic relationship. While it may be challenging, strive to maintain open and respectful communication with your ex-partner for the sake of your children.

Keep conversations focused on the needs of your children and avoid getting drawn into arguments or conflicts. Use clear and concise language, and try to remain calm and composed, even if your ex-partner becomes confrontational or hostile.

Consider using written communication, such as email or text messages, to minimize direct conflict and provide a record of your interactions. This can be helpful if disputes arise or if you need to document any concerning behavior.

Setting clear boundaries is crucial when co-parenting in a toxic relationship. Boundaries help protect both you and your children from the negative effects of toxic behavior. Establishing and enforcing boundaries can help create a healthier co-parenting dynamic.

Communicate your boundaries to your ex-partner in a calm and assertive manner. Be clear about what behaviors are unacceptable and the consequences for crossing those boundaries. Stick to your boundaries consistently and seek support from a therapist or counselor if you need help establishing and maintaining them.

Co-parenting in a toxic relationship can be emotionally challenging and overwhelming. It is essential to seek support from trusted friends, family members, or professionals who can provide guidance and understanding.

Consider joining a support group for individuals co-parenting in toxic relationships. These groups can offer a safe space to share experiences, gain insights, and receive support from others who are going through similar challenges.

Additionally, individual therapy can be beneficial for both you and your children. A therapist can help you navigate the complexities of co-parenting in a toxic relationship, manage your emotions, and develop coping strategies.

Taking care of yourself is crucial when co-parenting in a toxic relationship. It is essential to prioritize your physical, emotional, and mental well-being to ensure that you can be the best parent possible for your children.

Engage in activities that bring you joy and help you relax. Practice self-care regularly, whether it's through exercise, meditation, hobbies, or spending time with loved ones. Take breaks when needed and allow yourself to recharge.
Remember that by taking care of yourself, you are better equipped to handle the challenges of co-parenting in a toxic relationship and provide a healthy environment for your children.

If communication and co-parenting conflicts become unmanageable, consider seeking professional mediation. A mediator can help facilitate productive discussions between you and your ex-partner, allowing for more effective co-parenting.

Mediation provides a neutral and safe space for both parties to express their concerns and work towards finding mutually agreeable solutions. A mediator can help you navigate difficult conversations, establish guidelines, and develop a co-parenting plan that prioritizes the well-being of your children.

In a toxic co-parenting relationship, it is essential to document any concerning incidents or behaviors. Keep a record of any instances of abusive or harmful behavior, including dates, times, and descriptions of what occurred.

Documenting incidents can serve as evidence if legal action becomes necessary or if you need to demonstrate patterns of behavior to professionals involved in your children's lives, such as therapists or lawyers.

Remember to keep these records in a safe and secure location, away from the reach of your ex-partner. Consider making copies or storing them digitally to ensure their preservation.
While co-parenting in a toxic relationship can be challenging, it is essential to focus on the positive aspects of your children's lives. Celebrate their achievements, support their interests, and create positive memories together.

By emphasizing the positive aspects of your co-parenting relationship, you can help create a healthier environment for your children. Encourage open communication, respect, and empathy, and model healthy behaviors for them to emulate.

Remember that your children deserve to grow up in a loving and supportive environment, even if it means navigating the challenges of co-parenting in a toxic relationship. By implementing these strategies, you can create a healthier co-parenting dynamic and prioritize the well-being of your children.

———

Seeking Legal Support and Mediation

When co-parenting in a toxic relationship, it is essential to understand the importance of seeking legal support and mediation. Dealing with a toxic ex-partner can be challenging, and having the right legal guidance and mediation can help ensure the well-being of both you and your children. This section will explore the benefits of seeking legal support and mediation in navigating co-parenting in a toxic relationship.

Seeking legal support is crucial when co-parenting in a toxic relationship. A skilled family law attorney can provide you with the necessary guidance and expertise to protect your rights and the best interests of your children. Here are some key reasons why seeking legal support is essential:

In a toxic co-parenting situation, it is crucial to establish clear parental rights and responsibilities. A family law attorney can help you navigate the legal process of establishing custody, visitation, and decision-making authority. They can ensure that your rights as a parent are protected and that the arrangements are in the best interests of your children.

A parenting plan is a written agreement that outlines the responsibilities and arrangements for co-parenting. It includes details such as custody schedules, visitation arrangements, decision-making processes, and communication guidelines. A family law attorney can help you create a comprehensive parenting plan that addresses the specific challenges of co-parenting in a toxic relationship. They can ensure that the plan is fair, reasonable, and in the best interests of your children.

Unfortunately, in some cases, toxic ex-partners may refuse to comply with court orders or engage in behaviors that violate the agreed-upon parenting plan. In such situations, seeking legal support is crucial to enforce court orders and hold the toxic ex-partner accountable for their actions. A family law attorney can help you navigate the legal process of enforcing court orders and ensure that your rights and the well-being of your children are protected.

As circumstances change over time, it may become necessary to modify custody and visitation arrangements. If you believe that the current arrangements are no longer in the best interests of your children due to the toxic behavior of your ex-partner, seeking legal support is essential. A family law attorney can help you navigate the process of modifying custody and visitation arrangements and ensure that the changes are fair and in the best interests of your children.

Mediation is a process in which a neutral third party helps facilitate communication and negotiation between co-parents. It can be an effective tool for resolving conflicts and reaching agreements in a toxic co-parenting relationship. Here are some benefits of seeking mediation:

In a toxic co-parenting relationship, communication can be challenging and often filled with conflict. Mediation provides a structured and safe environment for co-parents to communicate and express their concerns. The mediator helps facilitate productive communication and ensures that both parties have an opportunity to be heard. By improving communication, mediation can help reduce conflict and create a more cooperative co-parenting dynamic.

Mediation encourages co-parents to work together and find mutually agreeable solutions. The mediator helps guide the negotiation process and assists in finding common ground. By promoting cooperation and collaboration, mediation can help co-parents develop a more positive and constructive relationship, which ultimately benefits the well-being of their children.

Unlike court proceedings, mediation allows co-parents to have more control over the outcome. They can work together to create customized solutions that meet the unique needs of their family. This flexibility can be particularly beneficial in a toxic co-parenting relationship, where standard court orders may not adequately address the specific challenges and dynamics involved.

Mediation is generally a more cost-effective and time-efficient alternative to litigation. It avoids the lengthy court process and associated legal fees. By resolving conflicts through mediation, co-parents can save both time and money, allowing them to focus on the well-being of their children.

When seeking legal support and mediation, it is crucial to find professionals who specialize in family law and have experience dealing with toxic co-parenting relationships. Here are some tips for finding the right legal support and mediator:

Start by researching family law attorneys and mediators in your area who have experience in dealing with toxic co-parenting cases. Seek recommendations from trusted sources, such as friends, family, or support groups for individuals who have gone through similar situations.

Schedule consultations with potential family law attorneys and mediators to discuss your case and assess their expertise and approach. Ask about their experience in handling toxic co-parenting cases and their success rate in achieving favorable outcomes.

It is essential to find professionals with whom you feel comfortable and can trust. Co-parenting in a toxic relationship can be emotionally challenging, and having a supportive and understanding legal team and mediator can make a significant difference in your experience.

Consider the cost and affordability of legal support and mediation services. While it is essential to find professionals who are skilled and experienced, it is also crucial to ensure that their services are within your budget. Discuss fees and payment options during the consultation process.

Seeking legal support and mediation is crucial when co-parenting in a toxic relationship. Legal professionals can provide guidance and protection of your rights, while mediators can help facilitate communication and negotiation. By seeking the right legal support and mediation, you can navigate the challenges of co-parenting in a toxic relationship more effectively and ensure the well-being of both you and your children.

CHAPTER 10: BUILDING HEALTHY RELATIONSHIPS

Understanding Healthy Relationships

In order to build healthy relationships, it is important to first understand what constitutes a healthy relationship. A healthy relationship is one that is built on mutual respect, trust, and open communication. It is a relationship where both partners feel valued, supported, and safe. In a healthy relationship, there is a balance of power and both partners have the freedom to express themselves without fear of judgment or reprisal.

Healthy relationships are characterized by several key factors:

1. Mutual Respect: In a healthy relationship, both partners have a deep respect for each other's boundaries, opinions, and feelings. They value each other as individuals and treat each other with kindness and consideration.
2. Trust and Honesty: Trust is the foundation of

any healthy relationship. Partners in a healthy relationship are honest with each other and trust that their partner will do the same. They are reliable and can depend on each other.

3. Effective Communication: Healthy relationships thrive on open and honest communication. Partners are able to express their thoughts, feelings, and needs in a respectful manner. They actively listen to each other and work together to find solutions to problems.

4. Equality and Balance: Healthy relationships are built on a foundation of equality. Both partners have an equal say in decision-making and share responsibilities. There is a balance of power and neither partner dominates or controls the other.

5. Support and Encouragement: Partners in a healthy relationship support and encourage each other's personal growth and goals. They celebrate each other's successes and provide emotional support during challenging times.

6. Individuality and Independence: In a healthy relationship, both partners maintain their individuality and have their own interests, hobbies, and friendships. They respect each other's need for personal space and time alone.

7. Conflict Resolution: Healthy relationships have effective conflict resolution strategies. Partners are able to address conflicts in a calm and respectful manner, seeking compromise and finding solutions that work for both parties.

While it is important to understand the characteristics of healthy relationships, it is equally important to be aware of the red flags that may indicate a toxic relationship. Recognizing these red flags can help you identify potential issues early on and take steps to address them. Some common red flags to watch out for include:

1. Lack of Respect: If your partner consistently disrespects your boundaries, opinions, or feelings, it may be a sign of a toxic relationship. Disrespect can manifest in various ways, such as belittling, name-calling, or dismissing your thoughts and emotions.

2. Control and Manipulation: A toxic partner may exhibit controlling and manipulative behaviors. They may try to control your actions, decisions, or relationships with others. They may use guilt, threats, or coercion to get their way.

3. Lack of Trust and Honesty: Trust is essential in a healthy relationship. If your partner consistently lies, hides information, or breaks promises, it can erode trust and create a toxic dynamic.

4. Poor Communication: Communication is the cornerstone of a healthy relationship. If your partner consistently avoids or dismisses your attempts to communicate, or if they resort to yelling, name-calling, or other forms of verbal abuse, it may be a sign of a toxic relationship.

5. Power Imbalance: In a healthy relationship, power is shared equally between partners. However, in a toxic relationship, one partner may exert control and dominance over the other. This can manifest in various ways, such as making all the decisions, controlling finances, or isolating the other partner from friends and family.

6. Emotional or Physical Abuse: Any form of abuse, whether emotional or physical, is a clear indication of a toxic relationship. Abuse can take many forms, including insults, threats, intimidation, physical violence, or sexual coercion. It is important to seek help and support if you are experiencing abuse in your relationship.

7. Lack of Support and Encouragement: In a healthy relationship, partners support and encourage each other's personal growth and goals. If your partner consistently undermines your aspirations, belittles your achievements, or discourages you from pursuing your dreams, it may be a sign of a toxic relationship.

Building healthy relationships requires effort and commitment from both partners. Here are some key strategies to foster a healthy relationship:

1. Open and Honest Communication: Foster open and honest communication by actively listening to your partner, expressing your thoughts and feelings respectfully, and being receptive to feedback.
2. Respect and Empathy: Treat your partner with respect and empathy, valuing their opinions, feelings, and boundaries. Practice active empathy by putting yourself in their shoes and trying to understand their perspective.
3. Establish Boundaries: Set clear boundaries and respect each other's boundaries. Boundaries help create a sense of safety and autonomy within the relationship.
4. Conflict Resolution: Learn healthy conflict resolution strategies, such as active listening, compromise, and finding win-win solutions. Avoid resorting to yelling, name-calling, or other forms of verbal or physical abuse.
5. Support and Encouragement: Support and encourage each other's personal growth and goals. Celebrate each other's successes and provide emotional support during challenging times.
6. Quality Time and Intimacy: Make time for each other and nurture intimacy in your relationship. Engage in

activities that you both enjoy and prioritize quality time together.

7. Continual Growth and Learning: Relationships are dynamic and require continual growth and learning. Be open to personal growth and self-reflection, and encourage your partner to do the same.

Remember, building a healthy relationship takes time and effort from both partners. It is important to be patient, understanding, and willing to work through challenges together. If you find yourself in a toxic relationship, it is crucial to seek support and take steps to protect your well-being.

Red Flags to Watch Out For

Recognizing red flags in a relationship is crucial for identifying whether it is healthy or toxic. While every relationship has its ups and downs, it is important to be aware of certain warning signs that may indicate a toxic dynamic. By being vigilant and observant, you can protect yourself from entering or staying in a harmful relationship. Here are some red flags to watch out for:

In a healthy relationship, both partners should be treated with respect and viewed as equals. However, in a toxic relationship, one partner may consistently disrespect the other, belittle their opinions, or dismiss their feelings. This lack of respect and equality can manifest in various ways, such as constant criticism, humiliation, or controlling behavior. If you notice a consistent pattern of disrespect, it may be a red flag indicating a toxic relationship.

While it is normal to feel a certain level of jealousy in a relationship, excessive jealousy and possessiveness can be signs of toxicity. If your partner constantly questions your whereabouts, monitors your activities, or becomes overly possessive, it can indicate a lack of trust and insecurity. Healthy relationships are built on trust and mutual respect, so it is important to address and communicate about any excessive jealousy or possessiveness.

Emotional manipulation is a common tactic used in toxic relationships. It involves the use of guilt, fear, or other negative emotions to control and manipulate the other person. Manipulative behaviors can include gaslighting, where the manipulator makes the victim doubt their own reality, or emotional blackmail, where the manipulator threatens to withhold love or affection. If you find yourself constantly feeling confused, guilty, or manipulated, it may be a sign of a toxic relationship.

Effective communication is the foundation of a healthy relationship. In a toxic relationship, however, communication may be lacking or ineffective. One partner may consistently avoid or shut down conversations, resorting to stonewalling or giving the silent treatment. This can lead to unresolved conflicts, misunderstandings, and a breakdown in emotional connection. If your partner consistently avoids open and honest communication, it may be a red flag indicating a toxic dynamic.

Controlling behavior is a significant red flag in a relationship. It can manifest in various ways, such as monitoring your phone or social media, dictating your clothing choices, isolating you from friends and family, or making decisions without your input. Healthy relationships are built on trust, autonomy, and mutual respect for each other's boundaries. If your partner consistently exhibits controlling behavior, it may be a sign of a toxic relationship.

In a healthy relationship, partners support and uplift each other. However, in a toxic relationship, one partner may constantly criticize, demean, or belittle the other. This constant negativity can erode self-esteem and create a toxic environment. If you find yourself constantly being put down or criticized by your partner, it may be a red flag indicating a toxic dynamic.

In a healthy relationship, both partners take responsibility for their actions and are willing to apologize and make amends when necessary. In a toxic relationship, however, one partner may consistently avoid taking accountability for their behavior and instead shift the blame onto the other person. This can create a cycle of blame and resentment, making it difficult to resolve conflicts and move forward. If your partner consistently avoids taking responsibility for their actions, it may be a sign of a toxic relationship.

A toxic partner may try to isolate you from your friends, family, or other supportive relationships. They may discourage you from spending time with loved ones, make you feel guilty for maintaining these connections, or create a sense of dependency on them. Isolation can make it easier for the toxic partner to exert control and manipulate the other person. If you find yourself becoming increasingly isolated from your support network, it may be a red flag indicating a toxic relationship.

In a healthy relationship, partners should feel emotionally stable and secure. However, in a toxic relationship, one partner may exhibit intense mood swings, going from extreme affection to anger or hostility without warning. This unpredictability can create a sense of fear and anxiety, as the other person never knows what to expect. If your partner's mood swings are causing emotional distress or fear, it may be a sign of a toxic dynamic.

Empathy and emotional support are essential components of a healthy relationship. In a toxic relationship, however, one partner may consistently lack empathy and fail to provide emotional support. They may dismiss or invalidate your feelings, minimize your experiences, or show a lack of understanding and compassion. If your partner consistently fails to provide emotional support or lacks empathy, it may be a red flag indicating a toxic relationship.

Recognizing these red flags is the first step in protecting yourself from a toxic relationship. It is important to trust your instincts and prioritize your well-being. If you notice any of these warning signs in your relationship, it may be necessary to seek support, set boundaries, or consider ending the relationship for your own emotional and mental health. Remember, you deserve to be in a healthy and nurturing relationship where you are respected, valued, and loved.

———

Effective Communication and Conflict Resolution

Effective communication and conflict resolution are essential components of building and maintaining healthy relationships. In a toxic relationship, communication often breaks down, leading to misunderstandings, resentment, and further damage to the relationship. Learning how to communicate effectively and resolve conflicts in a healthy manner is crucial for creating a safe and nurturing environment.

Communication is the foundation of any relationship. It is how we express our thoughts, feelings, and needs to others. In a healthy relationship, effective communication allows both partners to feel heard, understood, and valued. It fosters trust, intimacy, and connection.

In a toxic relationship, communication becomes distorted, manipulative, and hurtful. Toxic partners may use communication as a tool for control, domination, and manipulation. They may engage in tactics such as gaslighting, invalidating, or stonewalling, which further erode the trust and emotional safety in the relationship.

1. Active Listening: Active listening involves fully focusing on and understanding what the other person is saying. It requires giving your full attention, maintaining eye contact, and avoiding distractions. Practice empathy and try to see things from the other person's perspective.

2. Use "I" Statements: When expressing your thoughts and feelings, use "I" statements instead of "you" statements. For example, instead of saying, "You always make me feel worthless," say, "I feel hurt and devalued when certain things happen."

3. Express Yourself Clearly: Be clear and concise when expressing your thoughts and feelings. Avoid using vague or ambiguous language that can lead to misunderstandings. Use specific examples to illustrate your point.

4. Avoid Blaming and Criticizing: Instead of blaming or criticizing the other person, focus on expressing how their behavior or actions make you feel. Use non-judgmental language and avoid attacking their character.

5. Validate and Acknowledge: Validate the other person's feelings and experiences. Show empathy and understanding. Acknowledge their perspective, even if you disagree with it. This helps create an atmosphere of mutual respect and understanding.

6. Take Responsibility for Your Actions: If you have made a mistake or hurt the other person, take responsibility for your actions. Apologize sincerely and make amends if necessary. This demonstrates your commitment to the relationship and shows that you value the other person's feelings.

7. Practice Non-Defensive Communication: Instead of becoming defensive or reactive when faced with criticism or conflict, practice non-defensive

communication. Stay calm, listen to the other person's concerns, and respond in a non-confrontational manner.

8. Set Boundaries: Clearly communicate your boundaries and expectations in the relationship. This helps establish a framework for healthy communication and ensures that both partners feel respected and safe.

Conflict is a natural part of any relationship. However, in healthy relationships, conflicts are resolved in a respectful and constructive manner. Here are some strategies for effective conflict resolution:

1. Choose the Right Time and Place: Find a suitable time and place to discuss the issue at hand. Avoid discussing sensitive topics when you or your partner are tired, stressed, or distracted. Create a safe and comfortable environment for open and honest communication.

2. Stay Calm and Respectful: During a conflict, it's important to stay calm and respectful. Avoid raising your voice, using derogatory language, or resorting to personal attacks. Focus on the issue at hand and express your thoughts and feelings in a constructive manner.

3. Listen and Validate: Give your partner the opportunity to express their thoughts and feelings. Listen actively and validate their perspective. Show empathy and understanding, even if you disagree. This helps create an atmosphere of mutual respect and cooperation.

4. Find Common Ground: Look for areas of agreement and common ground. Focus on finding solutions that benefit both partners. Collaborate and brainstorm together to find creative and mutually satisfying

resolutions.

5. Compromise and Negotiate: In healthy relationships, both partners are willing to compromise and negotiate. Be open to finding middle ground and be willing to make concessions. Seek win-win solutions that address the needs and concerns of both partners.

6. Seek Mediation if Necessary: If you find it difficult to resolve conflicts on your own, consider seeking the help of a professional mediator or therapist. A neutral third party can provide guidance and facilitate productive communication.

7. Learn from Conflict: Conflict can be an opportunity for growth and learning. Reflect on the conflict and identify any patterns or underlying issues that may need to be addressed. Use the conflict as a chance to deepen your understanding of each other and strengthen your relationship.

Remember, effective communication and conflict resolution are skills that can be learned and developed over time. By practicing these strategies, you can create a healthier and more fulfilling relationship based on open, honest, and respectful communication.

Nurturing Trust and Intimacy

Trust and intimacy are essential components of a healthy and fulfilling relationship. However, in the aftermath of a toxic relationship, it can be challenging to rebuild these foundations. The scars left by toxic relationships can make it difficult to trust others and open up emotionally. But with time, patience, and self-reflection, it is possible to nurture trust and intimacy in future relationships. In this section, we will explore some strategies to help you rebuild trust and cultivate intimacy in a healthy and loving way.

Trust is the foundation upon which all relationships are built. It is the belief that someone is reliable, honest, and has your best interests at heart. In a toxic relationship, trust is often shattered due to lies, betrayal, and manipulation. Rebuilding trust requires a conscious effort from both partners.

To nurture trust, it is crucial to communicate openly and honestly. Share your thoughts, feelings, and concerns with your partner, and encourage them to do the same. Transparency and vulnerability are key in rebuilding trust. Be patient with each other and give yourselves time to heal from past wounds.

Emotional intimacy is the deep connection and understanding between two individuals. It involves sharing your innermost thoughts, fears, and dreams with your partner. In a toxic relationship, emotional intimacy is often stifled or manipulated. Rebuilding emotional intimacy requires creating a safe and supportive environment.

To nurture emotional intimacy, practice active listening. Give your partner your full attention when they are speaking and validate their feelings. Show empathy and understanding, even if you may not agree with their perspective. Create opportunities for deep conversations and encourage vulnerability. By fostering a safe space for emotional expression, you can gradually rebuild emotional intimacy.

Physical intimacy is an important aspect of a romantic relationship. However, in a toxic relationship, physical intimacy can become distorted or used as a tool for control. Rebuilding physical intimacy requires establishing boundaries and consent.

Start by having open and honest conversations about your desires, boundaries, and comfort levels. Take things slow and allow yourself to feel safe and secure before engaging in physical intimacy. It is essential to prioritize consent and respect each other's boundaries at all times. By rebuilding physical intimacy on a foundation of trust and respect, you can create a healthy and fulfilling connection.

1. Practice Effective Communication: Communication is the cornerstone of any healthy relationship. Be open, honest, and transparent with your partner. Express your needs, desires, and concerns, and encourage them to do the same. Effective communication builds trust and fosters intimacy.

2. Be Reliable and Consistent: Consistency is crucial in building trust. Show up for your partner consistently and follow through on your commitments. Be reliable and dependable, as this will help your partner feel secure and build trust over time.

3. Respect Boundaries: Respecting each other's boundaries is essential in nurturing trust and intimacy. Communicate and establish clear boundaries, and honor them. Respect your partner's need for personal space and privacy, and encourage them to do the same.

4. Practice Forgiveness: Forgiveness is a vital part of rebuilding trust. Let go of past hurts and resentments, and work towards forgiveness. Remember that forgiveness is a process and may take time. Be patient with yourself and your partner as you navigate this journey together.

5. Seek Professional Help if Needed: If you find it challenging to rebuild trust and intimacy on your own, consider seeking the help of a therapist or counselor. They can provide guidance, support, and tools to help you navigate the healing process.

Remember, rebuilding trust and intimacy takes time and effort from both partners. Be patient with yourself and your partner as you work towards creating a healthy and loving relationship. With dedication and a commitment to growth, you can nurture trust and intimacy and create a fulfilling and lasting connection.

CHAPTER 11: SELF-LOVE AND SELF-CARE

The Importance of Self-Love

Self-love is a fundamental aspect of our overall well-being and happiness. It is the foundation upon which we build healthy relationships, make positive choices, and navigate life's challenges. In the context of toxic relationships, self-love becomes even more crucial. It is the key to recognizing and healing from unhealthy relationships, as well as preventing them from reoccurring in the future.

Self-love is often misunderstood as being selfish or self-centered. However, it is quite the opposite. Self-love is about having a deep and genuine appreciation for oneself. It involves accepting and embracing all aspects of who we are, including our strengths, weaknesses, and imperfections. It means treating ourselves with kindness, compassion, and respect.

When we practice self-love, we prioritize our own well-being and happiness. We understand that taking care of ourselves is not only essential but also enables us to show up fully in our relationships and other areas of life. Self-love is the foundation upon which we build a healthy sense of self-worth and self-esteem.

Self-care is an integral part of self-love. It involves engaging in activities that nurture and nourish our physical, emotional, and mental well-being. Self-care is not selfish; it is a necessary practice that allows us to recharge, rejuvenate, and replenish ourselves.
In the context of toxic relationships, self-care becomes even more critical. It is a way to protect ourselves from the negative effects of toxic dynamics and regain our sense of self. By prioritizing self-care, we create boundaries that prevent us from being consumed by the toxicity of the relationship.

Self-care can take many forms, and it is essential to find what works best for you. It could be engaging in activities that bring you joy and relaxation, such as reading, taking walks in nature, practicing yoga, or spending time with loved ones. It could also involve setting aside time for self-reflection, journaling, or seeking professional help.

Self-compassion is a vital aspect of self-love. It involves treating ourselves with kindness, understanding, and empathy, especially during challenging times. In the context of toxic relationships, self-compassion allows us to acknowledge our pain and validate our experiences without judgment or self-blame.

Cultivating self-compassion involves recognizing that we are human and that we all make mistakes. It means offering ourselves the same level of compassion and understanding that we would extend to a dear friend or loved one. Self-compassion allows us to heal from the wounds inflicted by toxic relationships and move forward with kindness and forgiveness towards ourselves.

Self-love is not a destination; it is a lifelong journey of personal growth and self-improvement. Embracing personal growth means being open to learning, evolving, and becoming the best version of ourselves. It involves taking responsibility for our own happiness and actively working towards creating a life that aligns with our values and aspirations.

In the context of toxic relationships, personal growth is essential for breaking free from the patterns and dynamics that kept us trapped. It requires us to examine our beliefs, behaviors, and choices, and make conscious efforts to change what no longer serves us. Personal growth empowers us to create healthier boundaries, make better relationship choices, and cultivate fulfilling connections.

Embracing personal growth also involves seeking support and guidance from trusted individuals, such as therapists, coaches, or support groups. These resources can provide valuable insights, tools, and strategies to navigate the healing process and foster personal growth.

Self-love is the cornerstone of recognizing and healing from toxic relationships. It involves practicing self-care, cultivating self-compassion, and embracing personal growth. By prioritizing self-love, we empower ourselves to break free from unhealthy dynamics, rebuild our lives, and create fulfilling and healthy relationships.

Remember, you are worthy of love, respect, and happiness, and practicing self-love is the first step towards reclaiming your power and living a life free from toxicity.

———

Practicing Self-Care

Self-care is an essential aspect of healing and recovering from a toxic relationship. When you have been in an unhealthy and toxic relationship, it is crucial to prioritize your well-being and take care of yourself. Practicing self-care can help you regain your sense of self, rebuild your self-esteem, and create a foundation for a healthier future. In this section, we will explore various self-care practices that can support your healing journey.

Taking care of your physical health is an integral part of self-care. When you have been in a toxic relationship, you may have neglected your physical well-being. Now is the time to focus on nurturing your body and giving it the care it deserves. Here are some self-care practices to consider:

1. Exercise: Engaging in regular physical activity can help release stress, boost your mood, and improve your overall well-being. Find an exercise routine that you enjoy, whether it's going for a walk, practicing yoga, or joining a fitness class.
2. Eating nutritious meals: Fueling your body with healthy and nourishing food is essential for your physical and mental well-being. Aim to incorporate a balanced diet rich in fruits, vegetables, whole grains, and lean proteins.
3. Getting enough sleep: Restful sleep is crucial for your body's recovery and rejuvenation. Establish a bedtime routine that promotes relaxation and ensures you get enough sleep each night.
4. Taking care of your appearance: Paying attention to your personal grooming and appearance can help boost your self-confidence and self-esteem. Take the time to dress in a way that makes you feel good about yourself and practice good hygiene.

Emotional self-care is vital for healing from a toxic relationship. It involves acknowledging and processing your emotions, practicing self-compassion, and engaging in activities that bring you joy and fulfillment. Here are some self-care practices to nurture your emotional well-being:

1. Journaling: Writing down your thoughts and feelings can be a therapeutic way to process your emotions and gain clarity. Consider keeping a journal where you can freely express yourself without judgment.
2. Engaging in hobbies and interests: Rediscover activities that bring you joy and make you feel alive. Whether it's painting, playing an instrument, gardening, or dancing, find activities that allow you to express yourself and find solace.
3. Practicing mindfulness and meditation: Mindfulness and meditation can help you cultivate a sense of inner peace and calm. Take a few moments each day to practice deep breathing, meditation, or mindfulness exercises to ground yourself and reduce stress.
4. Seeking therapy or counseling: Professional support can be immensely beneficial in your healing journey. Consider seeking therapy or counseling to work through the emotional wounds and gain insights into your experiences.

Building healthy relationships and surrounding yourself with a supportive network is crucial for your well-being. Here are some self-care practices to cultivate healthy relationships and support systems:

1. Setting boundaries: Establishing clear boundaries is essential to protect your emotional well-being and prevent toxic dynamics from infiltrating your life. Communicate your needs and limits to others and enforce them consistently.
2. Nurturing positive relationships: Invest your time and energy in relationships that uplift and support you. Surround yourself with people who genuinely care about your well-being and encourage your personal growth.

3. Joining support groups: Connecting with others who have experienced similar toxic relationships can provide validation, understanding, and a sense of belonging. Consider joining support groups or online communities where you can share your experiences and receive support.

4. Seeking professional guidance: If you find it challenging to navigate relationships or establish healthy boundaries, seeking guidance from a therapist or counselor can provide you with valuable insights and tools.

Self-compassion is a crucial aspect of self-care, especially when healing from a toxic relationship. It involves treating yourself with kindness, understanding, and acceptance. Here are some self-care practices to cultivate self-compassion:

1. Positive self-talk: Challenge negative self-talk and replace it with positive and affirming statements. Remind yourself of your worth, strengths, and resilience.

2. Self-forgiveness: Let go of self-blame and forgive yourself for any perceived mistakes or shortcomings. Understand that you did the best you could with the knowledge and resources you had at the time.

3. Practicing self-acceptance: Embrace yourself fully, including your flaws and imperfections. Accept that you are a work in progress and that growth and healing take time.

4. Engaging in self-soothing activities: Find activities that bring you comfort and soothe your soul. It could be taking a warm bath, reading a book, listening to calming music, or practicing relaxation techniques.

Remember, self-care is not selfish; it is a necessary part of your healing journey. By prioritizing your well-being and practicing self-care, you are taking important steps towards reclaiming your life and creating a healthier and happier future.

———

Cultivating Self-Compassion

Self-compassion is a vital aspect of healing and recovering from a toxic relationship. When we have been in an unhealthy and toxic relationship, it is common to experience feelings of self-blame, shame, and low self-worth. Cultivating self-compassion allows us to treat ourselves with kindness, understanding, and acceptance, which is crucial for our emotional well-being and growth.

Self-compassion is the practice of extending compassion to oneself in times of suffering, pain, or failure. It involves treating ourselves with the same kindness, care, and understanding that we would offer to a loved one who is going through a difficult time. Self-compassion is not about self-pity or self-indulgence; instead, it is about acknowledging our pain and suffering with a sense of empathy and understanding.

Cultivating self-compassion can have numerous benefits for individuals who have experienced a toxic relationship. Here are some of the ways in which self-compassion can support healing and growth:

1. Reduced self-blame: Self-compassion helps us recognize that we are not solely responsible for the toxicity in the relationship. It allows us to let go of self-blame and understand that we deserve love and respect.
2. Increased self-acceptance: Self-compassion encourages us to accept ourselves as we are, flaws and all. It helps us embrace our imperfections and recognize that we are worthy of love and belonging.

3. Improved emotional well-being: By practicing self-compassion, we can develop healthier coping mechanisms for dealing with difficult emotions. It allows us to be gentle with ourselves and provide the emotional support we need during challenging times.

4. Enhanced resilience: Self-compassion helps us bounce back from setbacks and challenges. It fosters a sense of inner strength and resilience, enabling us to navigate future difficulties with greater ease.

5. Greater self-care: Cultivating self-compassion encourages us to prioritize our well-being and engage in self-care practices. It reminds us to set boundaries, prioritize our needs, and engage in activities that bring us joy and fulfillment.

Practicing self-compassion is a skill that can be developed over time. Here are some strategies to cultivate self-compassion in your life:

1. Mindful self-awareness: Begin by becoming aware of your thoughts and emotions without judgment. Notice when you are being self-critical or harsh towards yourself. Practice observing your thoughts and emotions with curiosity and compassion.

2. Self-kindness: Treat yourself with kindness and understanding. When you make a mistake or experience a setback, respond to yourself with words of encouragement and support. Remind yourself that everyone makes mistakes and that it is a part of being human.

3. Self-acceptance: Embrace your imperfections and accept yourself as you are. Recognize that you are worthy of love and belonging, regardless of your flaws or past experiences. Practice self-acceptance by focusing on your strengths and celebrating your achievements.

4. Self-soothing: Develop self-soothing techniques to comfort yourself during difficult times. This could include engaging in activities that bring you joy, practicing relaxation techniques such as deep breathing or meditation, or seeking support from trusted friends or family members.

5. Self-compassionate self-talk: Pay attention to the way you speak to yourself. Replace self-critical thoughts with self-compassionate and supportive statements. Treat yourself as you would treat a close friend or loved one who is going through a challenging time.

6. Self-forgiveness: Let go of self-blame and forgive yourself for any mistakes or shortcomings. Recognize that you are human and that making mistakes is a part of the learning and growth process. Practice self-forgiveness by acknowledging your mistakes, learning from them, and moving forward with compassion.

7. Self-care: Prioritize self-care activities that nourish your mind, body, and soul. Engage in activities that bring you joy, relaxation, and fulfillment. This could include practicing yoga, spending time in nature, journaling, or engaging in creative pursuits.

Cultivating self-compassion is an essential part of the personal growth journey after a toxic relationship. It allows us to heal from past wounds, develop a healthier relationship with ourselves, and create a more fulfilling and loving life. By embracing self-compassion, we can let go of self-judgment and embrace our inherent worthiness. Remember, you deserve love, kindness, and compassion – from others and from yourself.

———

Embracing Personal Growth

Personal growth is an essential aspect of healing from a toxic relationship. When we find ourselves in unhealthy relationships, it can be easy to lose sight of our own personal growth and development. However, embracing personal growth is crucial for moving forward and creating a healthier and happier life.

Personal growth is the process of self-improvement and self-development. It involves gaining self-awareness, learning new skills, and making positive changes in our lives. In the context of toxic relationships, personal growth is especially important because it allows us to break free from negative patterns and behaviors and create a better future for ourselves.

Embracing personal growth after a toxic relationship is essential for several reasons:

1. Breaking free from the past: Personal growth helps us let go of the pain and trauma of the toxic relationship. It allows us to release negative emotions and move forward with a fresh perspective.
2. Building resilience: Personal growth helps us develop resilience, which is the ability to bounce back from adversity. By focusing on our personal growth, we can strengthen our emotional well-being and become more resilient in the face of challenges.
3. Creating a positive mindset: Personal growth encourages us to adopt a positive mindset. It helps us shift our focus from the negative aspects of the toxic relationship to the possibilities and opportunities that lie ahead.
4. Discovering our true selves: Toxic relationships often cause us to lose touch with our authentic selves. Personal growth allows us to reconnect with who we truly are and rediscover our passions, values, and goals.

Embracing personal growth after a toxic relationship is a journey that requires time, patience, and self-compassion. Here are some steps you can take to embrace personal growth:

1. Self-reflection: Take the time to reflect on your experiences in the toxic relationship. Ask yourself what lessons you have learned and how you can use those lessons to grow and evolve.

2. Set goals: Identify areas of your life that you would like to improve and set goals for yourself. These goals can be related to your career, relationships, health, or personal development. Setting goals gives you something to work towards and helps you stay focused on your personal growth.

3. Seek support: Surround yourself with a supportive network of friends, family, or a therapist who can provide guidance and encouragement on your personal growth journey. Having a support system can make a significant difference in your ability to embrace personal growth.

4. Learn new skills: Personal growth often involves acquiring new skills or knowledge. Take the opportunity to learn something new that interests you, whether it's a hobby, a language, or a professional skill. Learning new things can boost your confidence and open up new opportunities for personal growth.

5. Practice self-care: Self-care is an essential aspect of personal growth. Take care of your physical, emotional, and mental well-being by engaging in activities that nourish and rejuvenate you. This can include exercise, meditation, spending time in nature, or engaging in creative pursuits.

6. Challenge yourself: Personal growth requires stepping out of your comfort zone and facing your fears. Challenge yourself to take small steps towards

personal growth, whether it's trying something new, taking on a new responsibility, or confronting a fear. Each step you take will contribute to your personal growth and development.

7. Celebrate your progress: Acknowledge and celebrate your achievements along the way. Recognize the progress you have made and give yourself credit for the steps you have taken towards personal growth. Celebrating your progress will motivate you to continue on your journey.

Embracing personal growth after a toxic relationship often involves embracing change and transformation. Here are some key aspects to consider:

1. Letting go of the past: To embrace personal growth, it is essential to let go of the past and release any lingering attachments to the toxic relationship. This may involve forgiving yourself and your ex-partner, as well as practicing self-compassion.

2. Embracing new opportunities: Personal growth opens up new opportunities for happiness, fulfillment, and success. Embrace these opportunities with an open mind and a willingness to explore new paths.

3. Learning from mistakes: Personal growth involves learning from past mistakes and using them as stepping stones for personal development. Reflect on the patterns and behaviors that contributed to the toxic relationship and make a conscious effort to avoid repeating them in the future.

4. Cultivating self-love: Embracing personal growth requires cultivating self-love and self-acceptance. Treat yourself with kindness, compassion, and respect. Practice self-care and prioritize your own well-being.

5. Seeking continuous growth: Personal growth is an

ongoing process. Embrace the mindset of continuous growth and commit to lifelong learning and self-improvement. Stay open to new experiences, challenges, and opportunities for personal growth.

Remember, personal growth is a unique and individual journey. Embrace it at your own pace and in a way that feels authentic to you. By embracing personal growth, you can heal from the toxic relationship and create a life filled with happiness, fulfillment, and healthy relationships.

CHAPTER 12:
MOVING FORWARD
AND THRIVING

*Rebuilding Your Life After
a Toxic Relationship*

Recovering from a toxic relationship can be a challenging and transformative journey. It is important to remember that healing takes time and patience, but with the right support and strategies, you can rebuild your life and create a healthier, happier future. In this section, we will explore some key steps and considerations for rebuilding your life after a toxic relationship.

The first step in rebuilding your life after a toxic relationship is to acknowledge and accept your experience. It is common to feel a range of emotions such as anger, sadness, confusion, and even guilt. Allow yourself to feel these emotions and understand that they are a natural part of the healing process. Recognize that the toxic relationship was not your fault and that you deserve to move forward and find happiness.

Rebuilding your life after a toxic relationship can be

overwhelming, and it is important to seek support from trusted friends, family, or professionals. Surround yourself with people who believe in you and can provide emotional support. Consider joining support groups or seeking therapy to help you process your emotions and gain valuable insights into your experiences. Remember, you don't have to go through this journey alone.

Self-care is crucial during the healing process. Prioritize your physical, emotional, and mental well-being. Engage in activities that bring you joy and help you relax. This could include exercise, meditation, journaling, spending time in nature, or pursuing hobbies and interests. Taking care of yourself will not only aid in your healing but also help you regain a sense of self and rebuild your self-esteem.

Take time to reflect on the toxic relationship and identify any patterns or red flags that you may have missed. This self-reflection will help you gain insight into your own needs, boundaries, and values. Use this knowledge to set healthier boundaries and make more informed choices in future relationships. Remember, self-reflection is a powerful tool for personal growth and can help you break free from unhealthy patterns.

Rebuilding your life after a toxic relationship involves setting goals and creating a vision for your future. Take some time to envision the life you want to live and the person you want to become. Set realistic and achievable goals that align with your values and aspirations. Whether it's pursuing a new career, developing new hobbies, or building stronger relationships, having a clear vision and goals will give you direction and motivation.

Rebuilding your life after a toxic relationship often requires embracing change and developing resilience. Understand that change is a natural part of life and that it can lead to growth and new opportunities. Embrace the challenges that come your way and view them as opportunities for personal development. Cultivate resilience by practicing self-compassion, staying positive, and seeking support when needed. Remember, you have the strength within you to overcome any obstacles and create a better future.

Forgiveness is a powerful tool for healing and moving forward. It is important to forgive yourself for any perceived mistakes or shortcomings in the toxic relationship. Understand that you did the best you could with the knowledge and resources you had at the time. Additionally, consider forgiving the person who caused you harm. Forgiveness does not mean condoning their actions but rather freeing yourself from the burden of anger and resentment. It allows you to let go and focus on your own healing and growth.

Practicing gratitude can have a profound impact on your healing journey. Take time each day to reflect on the things you are grateful for, no matter how small they may seem. This can help shift your focus from the negative aspects of the toxic relationship to the positive aspects of your life. Cultivating gratitude can also help you develop a more positive mindset and attract more positivity into your life.

If you find that you are struggling to rebuild your life after a toxic relationship, don't hesitate to seek professional help. A therapist or counselor can provide guidance, support, and tools to help you navigate the healing process. They can assist you in developing coping strategies, processing your emotions, and building resilience. Remember, reaching out for help is a sign of strength, and it can greatly accelerate your healing journey.

As you rebuild your life after a toxic relationship, celebrate your progress and achievements along the way. Recognize and acknowledge the steps you have taken to heal and grow. Celebrate even the smallest victories, as they are significant milestones on your journey. By celebrating your progress, you reinforce your resilience and remind yourself of your strength and ability to overcome adversity.

Rebuilding your life after a toxic relationship is a courageous and transformative process. It requires self-reflection, self-care, and the support of others. Remember to be patient with yourself and embrace the journey of healing and growth. With time, you will not only rebuild your life but also thrive in a healthier and more fulfilling future.

Setting Goals and Creating a Vision

Setting goals and creating a vision for your future is an essential part of moving forward and thriving after a toxic relationship. When you have experienced the pain and turmoil of a toxic relationship, it is crucial to take the time to reflect on your desires, dreams, and aspirations. By setting goals and creating a vision, you can regain control of your life and pave the way for a brighter and more fulfilling future.

Setting goals provides you with a sense of direction and purpose. It allows you to focus your energy and efforts on specific areas of your life that you want to improve or achieve. When you have clear goals, you are more likely to stay motivated, overcome obstacles, and make progress towards the life you envision for yourself.

In the aftermath of a toxic relationship, it is common to feel lost, confused, and uncertain about the future. Setting goals can help you regain a sense of stability and control. It allows you to shift your focus from the pain of the past to the possibilities of the future.

Before you can set meaningful goals, it is important to take the time to reflect on your values and passions. What truly matters to you? What brings you joy and fulfillment? By understanding your core values and passions, you can align your goals with what is truly important to you.

Consider the activities, hobbies, or interests that make you feel alive and fulfilled. Think about the values that guide your life, such as honesty, compassion, or personal growth. Reflecting on these aspects of yourself will help you create goals that are authentic and meaningful.

When setting goals, it is helpful to follow the SMART framework. SMART stands for Specific, Measurable, Achievable, Relevant, and Time-bound. By applying these criteria to your goals, you can ensure that they are clear, realistic, and actionable.

- Specific: Clearly define what you want to achieve. Instead of setting a vague goal like "be happier," specify what happiness means to you and how you will achieve it.
- Measurable: Establish criteria to measure your progress. This could be a specific number, a timeline, or a tangible outcome. Measurable goals allow you to track your progress and celebrate your achievements.
- Achievable: Set goals that are within your reach. While it is important to challenge yourself, setting unrealistic goals can lead to frustration and disappointment. Consider your current circumstances and resources when setting your goals.
- Relevant: Ensure that your goals align with your values, passions, and overall vision for your life. Setting goals that are meaningful to you will increase your motivation and commitment to achieving them.
- Time-bound: Set a deadline or timeline for achieving your goals. This creates a sense of urgency and helps you stay focused and accountable.

A vision board is a powerful tool for visualizing your goals and dreams. It is a collage of images, words, and symbols that represent the life you want to create for yourself. Creating a vision board can help you clarify your goals, stay motivated, and manifest your desires.

To create a vision board, gather magazines, newspapers, or printouts of images that resonate with your goals and aspirations. Cut out the images and words that inspire you and arrange them on a poster board or a piece of paper. You can also add personal photos, quotes, or affirmations that reflect your vision.

Place your vision board in a prominent place where you can see it every day. Take a few moments each day to visualize yourself living the life you desire. Allow the images and words on your vision board to inspire and motivate you as you work towards your goals.

Once you have set your goals and created a vision, it is important to break them down into smaller, manageable steps. Breaking down your goals into actionable tasks makes them less overwhelming and more achievable.

Start by identifying the specific actions or milestones that will lead you towards your goals. Then, create a timeline or schedule for completing these tasks. By taking small, consistent steps towards your goals, you will build momentum and make progress over time.

While setting goals and creating a vision is important, it is equally important to stay flexible and adapt as needed. Life is unpredictable, and circumstances may change along the way. Be open to adjusting your goals and strategies as necessary to stay aligned with your values and passions.

Remember that the journey towards your goals is just as important as the destination. Embrace the process of personal growth and self-discovery that comes with setting and pursuing your goals. Celebrate your achievements along the way and be kind to yourself when faced with setbacks or challenges.

Setting goals and creating a vision can be a challenging process, especially after experiencing a toxic relationship. It is important to seek support and accountability from trusted friends, family members, or professionals. Share your goals with someone who can provide encouragement, guidance, and accountability as you work towards them.

Consider joining a support group or seeking the help of a therapist or coach who specializes in healing from toxic relationships. They can provide valuable insights, tools, and support to help you navigate the process of setting goals and creating a vision for your future.

Remember, you have the power to create a life that is free from toxicity and filled with happiness and fulfillment. By setting goals and creating a vision, you are taking an important step towards reclaiming your life and thriving after a toxic relationship. Embrace the journey, stay committed to your goals, and believe in your ability to create the life you deserve.

———

Embracing Change and Resilience

Change is an inevitable part of life, and after coming out of a toxic relationship, it is crucial to embrace change and cultivate resilience. Moving forward and thriving requires a willingness to adapt, grow, and learn from past experiences. In this section, we will explore the importance of embracing change and building resilience as you rebuild your life after a toxic relationship.

Change can be intimidating, especially after going through a toxic relationship where stability and routine may have been disrupted. However, embracing change is essential for personal growth and creating a healthier future. Here are some strategies to help you embrace change:

1. Acceptance: Accept that change is a natural part of life and that it is necessary for personal growth. Recognize that change can bring new opportunities and a chance for a fresh start.
2. Open-mindedness: Be open to new experiences, ideas, and perspectives. Challenge yourself to step out of your comfort zone and explore different possibilities.
3. Flexibility: Cultivate flexibility and adaptability. Understand that things may not always go as planned, and being able to adjust your expectations and plans can help you navigate through change more effectively.
4. Positive mindset: Maintain a positive mindset and focus on the potential benefits that change can bring. Instead of dwelling on the past, look forward to the future and the opportunities it holds.
5. Self-reflection: Take time to reflect on your past experiences and identify areas where change is needed. This self-reflection will help you gain clarity on what you want to change and how you can make positive adjustments in your life.
6. Seek support: Surround yourself with a supportive network of friends, family, or a therapist who can provide guidance and encouragement as you navigate through change. Having a support system can make the process of embracing change feel less overwhelming.

Resilience is the ability to bounce back from adversity and overcome challenges. It is a crucial trait to develop after experiencing a toxic relationship. Building resilience will help you cope with setbacks, maintain a positive outlook, and thrive in the face of adversity. Here are some strategies to help you build resilience:

1. Self-care: Prioritize self-care activities that promote physical, emotional, and mental well-being. Engage in activities that bring you joy, relaxation, and rejuvenation. This will help you build emotional strength and resilience.

2. Develop a support system: Surround yourself with positive and supportive people who uplift and encourage you. Having a strong support system can provide a sense of belonging and help you navigate through difficult times.

3. Practice gratitude: Cultivate a mindset of gratitude by focusing on the positive aspects of your life. Regularly express gratitude for the things you have and the progress you have made. This will help shift your perspective and build resilience.

4. Set realistic goals: Set realistic and achievable goals for yourself. Break them down into smaller, manageable steps, and celebrate your progress along the way. This will help you build confidence and resilience as you accomplish each milestone.

5. Learn from setbacks: View setbacks as opportunities for growth and learning. Instead of dwelling on failures, reflect on what you can learn from them and how you can use those lessons to move forward. This mindset shift will help you build resilience and bounce back stronger.

6. Practice self-compassion: Be kind and compassionate towards yourself. Treat yourself with the same love and understanding you would offer to a friend. Acknowledge that healing takes time and that setbacks are a natural part of the process.

7. Develop problem-solving skills: Enhance your problem-solving skills by breaking down challenges into smaller, manageable parts. Identify potential

solutions and evaluate their pros and cons. This will help you approach problems with a more resilient mindset.

8. Maintain a positive outlook: Cultivate a positive outlook on life by focusing on the present moment and finding joy in the little things. Surround yourself with positive influences, engage in activities that bring you happiness, and practice positive affirmations.

Remember, building resilience takes time and effort. Be patient with yourself and celebrate your progress along the way. Embracing change and building resilience will empower you to create a fulfilling and healthy life after a toxic relationship.

———

Finding Happiness and Fulfillment

Finding happiness and fulfillment after a toxic relationship is a journey that requires self-reflection, healing, and personal growth. It is important to remember that you deserve to be happy and to live a life that is fulfilling and meaningful. While the process may be challenging at times, it is possible to move forward and create a life that brings you joy and satisfaction. In this section, we will explore some strategies and practices that can help you find happiness and fulfillment after a toxic relationship.

One powerful way to find happiness and fulfillment is by cultivating gratitude in your life. Gratitude is the practice of acknowledging and appreciating the positive aspects of your life, even in the face of challenges. After a toxic relationship, it can be easy to focus on the negative experiences and emotions. However, by shifting your focus to the things you are grateful for, you can begin to cultivate a more positive outlook.

Start by making a list of things you are grateful for each day. This can include simple things like a beautiful sunset, a supportive friend, or a delicious meal. By consciously acknowledging and appreciating these things, you can begin to shift your mindset and find happiness in the present moment.

Another key to finding happiness and fulfillment is by pursuing your passions and interests. After a toxic relationship, you may have lost touch with the things that bring you joy and fulfillment. Take some time to reflect on the activities and hobbies that you used to enjoy or that you have always wanted to try.

Make a list of these passions and interests and start incorporating them into your life. Whether it's painting, dancing, writing, or hiking, find ways to engage in activities that bring you joy. Not only will this help you rediscover your passions, but it will also provide a sense of fulfillment and purpose.

Building healthy relationships is essential for finding happiness and fulfillment. After a toxic relationship, it is important to surround yourself with people who support and uplift you. Seek out friendships and connections that are based on mutual respect, trust, and positivity.

Take the time to evaluate your current relationships and identify any toxic patterns or dynamics. Set boundaries with individuals who do not contribute positively to your life and prioritize relationships that bring you joy and fulfillment. Remember, healthy relationships are built on open communication, trust, and mutual support.

Self-care is a crucial aspect of finding happiness and fulfillment after a toxic relationship. It involves taking care of your physical, emotional, and mental well-being. Self-care looks different for everyone, so it's important to identify the activities and practices that nourish and rejuvenate you.

Some examples of self-care activities include taking a relaxing bath, practicing mindfulness or meditation, engaging in regular exercise, spending time in nature, or indulging in a hobby you enjoy. Prioritize self-care as a non-negotiable part of your routine and make time for activities that bring you joy and relaxation.

Setting realistic goals is an important step in finding happiness and fulfillment. After a toxic relationship, it can be easy to feel overwhelmed or unsure about the future. By setting goals, you can create a sense of direction and purpose in your life.

Start by identifying what you want to achieve in different areas of your life, such as career, relationships, personal growth, and health. Break these goals down into smaller, manageable steps and create a plan to work towards them. Celebrate your progress along the way and adjust your goals as needed.

Practicing mindfulness and self-reflection is a powerful tool for finding happiness and fulfillment. Mindfulness involves being fully present in the moment and observing your thoughts and emotions without judgment. By cultivating mindfulness, you can develop a deeper understanding of yourself and your needs.

Take time each day to engage in mindfulness practices such as meditation, deep breathing, or journaling. Use these practices to reflect on your experiences, emotions, and desires. By developing self-awareness, you can make conscious choices that align with your values and bring you closer to happiness and fulfillment.

Seeking support from others is crucial in finding happiness and fulfillment after a toxic relationship. Surround yourself with a supportive network of friends, family, or a therapist who can provide guidance, validation, and encouragement.

Consider joining support groups or seeking therapy to help you navigate the healing process. Connecting with others who have experienced similar situations can provide a sense of belonging and understanding. Remember, you do not have to go through this journey alone.

Forgiveness is a powerful practice that can help you find happiness and fulfillment. It involves letting go of resentment, anger, and bitterness towards yourself and others. Forgiveness does not mean condoning or forgetting the harm that was done, but rather freeing yourself from the emotional burden.

Take time to reflect on the past and the pain you have experienced. Practice self-compassion and extend forgiveness to yourself for any mistakes or perceived shortcomings. Similarly, consider forgiving the person who caused harm, not for their benefit, but for your own healing and growth.

Finally, finding happiness and fulfillment after a toxic relationship requires embracing new beginnings. It is an opportunity to redefine yourself, your values, and your priorities. Embrace the lessons you have learned and use them as stepping stones towards a brighter future.

Allow yourself to dream and envision the life you want to create. Embrace change and take small steps towards your goals. Remember, you have the power to create a life that is filled with happiness, fulfillment, and healthy relationships.

By implementing these strategies and practices, you can find happiness and fulfillment after a toxic relationship. Remember to be patient and kind to yourself throughout the process. Healing takes time, but with perseverance and self-compassion, you can create a life that is filled with joy, purpose, and love.